# Only Love Remains

## Dancing at the Edge of Extinction

D0063779

# Previous Works

2018 **Ms. Ladybug and Mr. Honeybee: A Love Story at the End of Time.**, Second edition, with Pauline Schneider. Woodthrush Productions, New York

2019 **Going Dark**, second edition. Woodthrush Productions, New York

2014 **Extinction Dialogues: How to Live with Death in Mind.** Baker C. and G.R. McPherson, Tayen Lane Publishing

2011 **Walking Away from Empire: A Personal Journey.** Publish America, Baltimore, Maryland

2009 **The Planner's Guide to Natural Resource Conservation: The Science of Land Development Beyond the Metropolitan Fringe.** Esparza, A.X. and G.R. McPherson, Springer, New York

2008 **Living with Fire: Fire Ecology and Policy for the Twenty-First Century.** Jensen, S.E. and G.R. McPherson. University of California Press, Berkeley

2006 **Academic Pursuits.** Brothers, Mac. Publish America, Baltimore, Maryland.

2006 **Letters to a Young Academic: Seeking Teachable Moments.** Rowman & Littlefield Education, Lanham, Maryland.

2004 **Killing the Natives: Has the American Dream Become a Nightmare?** Whitmore Publishing Company, Pittsburgh, Pennsylvania

2003 **Changing Precipitation Regimes and Terrestrial Ecosystems.** Weltzin, J.F. and G.R. McPherson. University of Arizona Press, Tucson

2003 **Applied Ecology and Natural Resource Management.** McPherson G.R. and S. DeStefano. Cambridge University Press, Cambridge, England.

1997 **Ecology and Management of North American Savannas.** University of Arizona Press, Tucson.

1990 **Glossary of Fire Management Terms Used in the United States.** McPherson G.R., D.D. Wade, and C.B. Phillips. Society of American Foresters, Bethesda, Maryland

# Only Love Remains

## Dancing at the Edge of Extinction

### Guy R. McPherson

Publisher,

Woodthrush Productions, New York

Cover design and art by Pauline Schneider

Back photo by Hanka Stratmann

ISBN: 978-1-7329631-3-9   hardback

ISBN: 978-1-7329631-0-8   paperback

## PUBLISHED BY

 **Woodthrush**

**Productions**

www.woodthrushproductions.com

# Table of Contents

# Preface

Essentially everybody knows that everybody dies. Essentially everybody knows life is short. Why do we act as if we will live forever? Why do we act as if Someday is just another day in the week?

Will we find our purpose? Will you find your purpose? Do you know what that means?

Throughout most of my career as a university scholar and teacher, I asked students to ponder the meaning of life, albeit not in the customary, larger-than-humanity sense. After discussing the notion of meaning and purpose, I would ask each student to write an epigraph after writing an obituary (most newspapers have replaced the latter with a notification of death written by family members). The epigraph came last because it is more difficult to write a compact version of one's life than to write a longer version.

The goal of this exercise was to determine what and who are important. If your epigraph reads, "Beloved Father and Poet," then clearly you aspire to fatherhood and poetry. Other cases are more complex, obviously. Surprisingly few college students have considered what they want to be when and if they "grow up."

A long time was required for me to find the meanings for my own existence. My purpose, my passion, the reason I try to live fully every day, is education.

I am a teacher. Teaching is not merely what I do. A teacher is who I am.

I should have known I was a teacher early in life when I was imploring my poor, 4-year-old sister to read from my copy of the *Dick and Jane* primers. I was only 6 years old myself. Truly finding my passion required leaving my passion of teaching behind when, at the age of 49 years, I voluntarily left active service as a tenured full professor at the University of Arizona. Shortly thereafter, on the homestead of my dreams in New Mexico, I realized too late that the homestead dream had become a nightmare. For years at a stretch, I was unable to interact frequently with young people. I had lost my way.

Mistakes are crucial to learning, of course, as most learning is experiential. If you are reading these words, you might have made a mistake or two of your own. If so, you are doubtless well on your way to uncovering your purpose in life. Perhaps this thin volume will help.

# Acknowledgments

This book was inspired by the thousands of people who hosted, organized, fed, and watered me during my speaking tours. I am grateful for the hundreds of people who have contributed financially to my tours and to food on my table. Most notable on both lists are my partner, sometimes co-author, and sometimes co-host Pauline Panagiotou Schneider, my beloved ex-wife Sheila Merrigan, and my friend, colleague, and co-host of NBL Radio Show, Kevin Hester.

My extensive writing, my years as host of the radio show I founded and created, more than ten years of blogging at Nature Bats Last, and my appearances for countless interviews and documentary films would have been impossible without the many supporters and followers of my work. I remain in your debt.

Insightful reviews of earlier drafts of this text came from readers of Nature Bats Last (guymcpherson.com). Additional critical reviews were graciously provided by Pauline Panagiotou Schneider, Paul Marcotte, and Ashley Blackburn. The final and most thorough proofreading edit was done in June, 2019 by our new, dear friend Jon Cypher.

# Introduction

*The weight of the world is love. Under the burden of solitude, under the burden of dissatisfaction.*

(Allen Ginsberg)

In many of my earlier writings, I have described how I have been seeking my life's purpose for a few decades. In one of the many recent attempts at this endeavor, at the request of a friend and colleague, I sought a picture of myself in my "element."

Sometimes even I find myself linguistically befuddled, and the search for my "element" has sent me straight to the Merriam-Webster dictionary for assistance. The relevant definition states element is, "the state or sphere natural or suited to a person or thing." As an example, it gives, "at school, she was in her element." As it turns out, so am I. At school, I am in my element.

Teaching suits me. Scholarship suits me. Delivering presentations suits me. Being interviewed suits me. Radical discussions, including facilitating the same, suits me just fine. What else? What more can I offer? What else suits me?

After pondering a few moments, I realized I am suited to being outdoors. I am suited to walking through the wilds of nature, as I have done my entire life, from grasslands to forests, and from deserts to jungles. I am suited to gratefully inhaling clean air as I observe undomesticated animals in their habitats. As it turned out, this is what my friend has in mind when she asked for the photograph.

I am glad my friend sent me on this quest. I am grateful to have pondered my element because it is closely related to the purposes I am pursuing during my time here on Earth.

Among the purposes of this book is to help you find your element. What "state or sphere [is] natural or suited to" you? How can you identify, seek, and find the reasons for your life?

Lacking passion, lacking purpose, the vast majority of people within this culture chase money for one reason: tradition. This is what they have always done. This is what the culture "tells" us to do. This is what "everybody" does in the struggle to stay alive and perhaps even remain comfortable.

Were it not for the frugal life I have conducted, along with the generosity of partners, friends, and supporters, I would have been living even closer to the monetary edge for the last several years.

My point: My message matters. At least it matters to me, considerably more than luxury. If I am to believe the positive messages I receive every day, then it matters to others as well.

Could my message matter to you? My answer is modified from a bumper sticker, ironically: Acceptance of abrupt climate change leading to near-term human extinction is optional, participation, however, is mandatory.

Cui bono? Who benefits from my message? Only the willing.

At the homestead I developed in southern New Mexico, I learned a lot about love. The primary motivation of the exercise, beyond heading off the Sixth Mass Extinction, was to extend my life as well as the life of my beloved wife. Brutally long days with a pick and shovel took over my previous life in the "ivory tower."

Thousands of hours were misspent performing rigorous manual labor, in the name of love.

It was in the high desert of New Mexico where I learned the unpleasantness of abandonment as my partner chose another path. I spent more than a thousand nights longing for an understanding companion. It was also here that I learned, with time, how to be pleasantly alone.

Hindsight is a marvelous teacher. Unfortunately, the lesson comes after the exam.

Now, too late to maintain those important long-term relationships, and many others, I know better than to throw myself into the breach. Now I do what I love and I encourage others to do the same. Sacrificing the work I loved for the woman I loved cost me both. As a result, I no longer recommend that approach. Balance and moderation are the two words that leap to mind.

Too little, too late. Mistakes have been made.

I worked diligently to retain my principles, and I still do. This is an approach I rarely observe in a culture characterized by indifference and mediocrity. For example, upon recognizing the costs of civilization, I could no longer contribute to the horrors. I voluntarily left active service in the academy, and led the way toward a simpler life, as described in one of my earlier books, *Walking Away from Empire*. Finally, when I learned about the extreme nature of global dimming, I recognized the error I had made.

Among the many errors that I made at the homestead in New Mexico were giving myself away and promulgating evidence. My love was returned, almost universally, with hatred and indifference rooted in ignorance. I have now learned, again too late for corrective action, the ugly inner nature that characterizes much of "civilized" humanity.

Rather than pursuing principles that put a relationship at risk, I now recommend doing what you love, for those who are able. After all, you cannot help anybody in the long run if you are not satisfied with your own life. Also, there is no longer a long run remaining for anybody reading these words. Love starts with you. Listen to the flight attendant: Put on your own mask first. This is not a selfish act, but an act of love for those around you who will need you to be okay to make sure they will be okay.

If extending your own personal time on Earth precludes the pursuit of doing what you love, then perhaps it is worth sacrificing your own personal satisfaction for a future with the one(s) you love. Extending a miserable life is not worth the effort, and living fully in the midst of loved ones is quite a pleasant tradeoff for an additional few weeks or months. Life is a complicated mess of many choices; some choices we make are doubtless antithetical to others. There are few easy answers in the pursuit of love, in the pursuit of excellence, in adherence to principle. If it is a hard choice, it is probably the right one.

Happiness for oneself is a foolish, temporary pursuit. Happiness is an outcome, a side effect, rather than a concrete item to be snared. Taking actions that one perceives to be within the realm of the pursuit of happiness *for another* is the very definition of insanity. Happiness is not Joy. This is a lesson I learned too late.

Perhaps my own journey will assist you in pursuing excellence and love. Safe journeys, fellow travelers, as long as habitat allows.

# Chapter 1: A Brief Overview

*In this age, the mere example of non-conformity, the mere refusal to bend the knee to custom, is itself a service. Precisely because the tyranny of opinion is such as to make eccentricity a reproach, it is desirable, in order to break through that tyranny, that people should be eccentric. Eccentricity has always abounded when and where strength of character has abounded; and the amount of eccentricity in a society has generally been proportional to the amount of genius, mental vigor, and moral courage which it contained. That so few now dare to be eccentric, marks the chief danger of the time.*

(John Stuart Mill)

What would you do if you had less than a decade to live? How would you act? How would you live?

What if it was less than 4 years?

What if it was less than a year?

What if it was a few months?

Would you live more fully every day? Every moment?

Would you prioritize your work differently? Or your relationships?

What is important to you? *Who* is important to you? Are you acting *now* as if these things and these beings are important?

This chapter serves as an introduction to the topic of near-term human extinction by focusing on five interrelated topics: (1) habitat for human animals, (2) civilization as a heat engine, (3) the Catch-22 of terminating civilization, (4) the Sixth Mass Extinction on Earth, and (5) how we respond to a terminal diagnosis. These topics are further articulated within additional chapters. I will include stories from my life to provide the reader with a sense of who I am and why I write books such as this one.

## *What is Habitat?*

According to the first definition in my Merriam-Webster online dictionary, habitat is, "the place or environment where a plant or animal naturally or normally lives and grows." This straightforward definition will suffice for the purposes of this text.

Being professor emeritus of conservation biology, I largely agree with this simplistic definition. Habitat is one of the three pillars of conservation biology, along with speciation and extinction. Speciation is the process of how, when, and with what ancestors a species comes into existence. For example, our favorite species, *Homo sapiens*, came into existence about

300,000 years ago, and is descended from earlier members of the genus *Homo* -- all of which are now extinct -- and is currently represented by more than 7.7 billion specimens. Some of these specimens were clever enough to choose their parents and their date and place of birth in a manner that allowed them to enjoy enormous privilege in their corporeal existence. The other 99%, not so much.

Extinction is the process by which a species meets its demise. So far, more than 99% of the species to appear on Earth have gone extinct, including half-a-dozen prior species in the genus *Homo*. Based on substantial evidence, our own species is headed into the abyss of extinction far sooner than most people realize.

Our species came into existence about 300,000 years ago. Coincidentally, millions of other species were evolving gradually due to changes in habitat. We rely on those myriad species for our own continued existence. If habitat changes too rapidly for species to adapt, they lose habitat and therefore go extinct. The previous five Mass Extinction Events represent examples of rapid changes in habitat that resulted in the extinction of prior species on Earth. This explains why habitat is such an important concept.

According to a paper published 18 July 2017 in *Earth System Dynamics,* senior-authored by James Hansen, the godfather of climate science, we have had humans on the planet only up to about 1.7° Celsius above the 1750 baseline (about 3.1°F), when the average planetary temperature was about 13.5°C (about 56°F). The paper in *Earth System Dynamics* concludes that the current planetary temperature is the highest planetary temperature at which *Homo sapiens* have been present on Earth. As a result, I suspect we are very near the maximum global-average temperature at which we will have habitat for humans on Earth, although we have not yet gone extinct so we do not know the maximum temperature at which this will occur. Earth is currently at least 1.7°C above the 1750 baseline (i.e., about 3.1°F above the 1750 baseline). No species persists long without habitat, not even the clever ones.

A synthetic paper written by Oliver Tickell and published in the *Guardian* on August 11, 2008, concluded via headline, "On a planet 4°C hotter, all we can prepare for is extinction." That 4°C number seems a tad high to me. I doubt there will be a tree on the planet, or much other complex life, with a rapid rise to 17.5°C (about 64°F). The article by Tickell goes on to explain that humans will persist up to 6°C above the 1750 baseline, thus about 19.5°C (about 67°F). I would be shocked. However, we do not know, because we have never experienced Earth with humans at anywhere close to 4°C above baseline, much less at 6°C above baseline, about 19.5°C (about 67°F).

# Civilization as a Heat Engine

Dr. Tim Garrett is a professor of atmospheric sciences at the University of Utah. He has been studying the thermodynamics of civilization for several years and wrote the signature paper on the topic in 2007. In that and subsequent papers, Garrett concluded that civilization itself is a heat engine. His initial paper on the topic was submitted in 2007, rejected by some ten journals, and finally accepted for publication in the prestigious journal *Climatic Change* in 2009 by courageous editor Steve Schneider during his final months on Earth. The paper ultimately was printed in February, 2011. The initial paper is supported by subsequent papers that point out that the heat engine of civilization can be stopped only when civilization collapses. This conclusion is based on the Laws of Thermodynamics.

Civilization is a tricky subject, so I will clarify what it means, from the perspective of Garrett and most other sane people. Civilization refers to the set of living arrangements into which most of us were born and to which we have all become accustomed. The collapse of civilization means no fuel at the filling stations, no food at the grocery stores, and no water pouring out of the municipal taps. This civilization, industrial civilization, is like all previous versions of civilization in that it depends upon the production, storage, and distribution of grains at a considerable scale. Without storing food, there is no other means by which humans can go into population overshoot.

Civilizations first arose a few thousand years ago in more than half-a-dozen places around the globe. No civilization came into being for the first 2.8 million years of the genus *Homo*, or for about the first 300,000 years of the species *Homo sapiens*, and then, suddenly, civilizations were popping up like trolls on YouTube. People within these early civilizations discovered grains such as maize and wheat, thus enabling humans to survive through droughts and other environmental inconveniences. Large-scale production and storage of grains also allowed control of the local food supply, hence control of the people. Thus did the sociopaths assume control.

Why did several civilizations arise essentially simultaneously a few thousand years ago? Apparently, the answer to this question is found within the global-average temperature of the planet. Coming out of the last Ice Age, the global-average planetary temperature rose from 12° Celsius (about 54°F) to about 13.5°C (about 56°F). More importantly, planetary temperature *stabilized* at that point. This relatively cool and stable temperature allowed grains to be grown in sufficient quantities to allow the development of cities. The word "city" shares the same root as civilization, *Civitas*, and the building of cities is the very definition of civilization. After all, cities allow human-population overshoot, initially locally and ultimately globally, because they depend upon surrounding areas for the delivery of clean air, potable water, healthy food, and the wood, bricks, and mortar from which structures are created.

Not only is civilization a heat engine (even if the civilization is powered by "renewable" energy) but each civilization trashes the planet to provide conveniences for city-dwellers. Consider, for example, the 200 or so species being driven to extinction every day, the fouling of the air, the pollution of the waters, the utter destruction of the soil, and the many other undesirable outcomes of this version of civilization.

The story we tell ourselves about ourselves - to use one definition of civilization - is filled with contradictions. This civilization, like others, is characterized by endemic racism, endemic misogyny, endemic monetary disparity leading to poverty, overshoot of the human population, accelerating the extinction of non-human species, and various other undesirable characteristics. Unlike other civilizations, this version is characterized by the infinite-growth paradigm, nuclear materials sufficient to cause our own extinction via multi-generational horrors resulting from lethal mutations, and now a new and also much quicker means to our end that no one is talking about: global dimming, otherwise known as the "aerosol masking effect."

# *Global Dimming, the Catch-22 of Human Extinction*

Civilization is a heat engine that is in the process of killing all life on Earth. Unfortunately, turning off the civilization loved by techno-nerdites and those of us born into relative privilege destroys most complex life on the planet, even faster than keeping it running. Allow me to explain, albeit briefly.

As most people know, industrial civilization puts into the atmosphere greenhouse gases such as carbon dioxide, methane, and about 40 others. These greenhouse gases (GHG) act as "blankets" to hold the heat provided by the sun close to Earth. Very inconveniently, industrial activity also produces particulates, (otherwise known as pollutants) that ironically serve as an "umbrella" above the blanket of GHG and thus, in a bizarre twist of fate, protect the planet from incoming sunlight that might further warm those gasses. According to a paper by Levy and colleagues that appeared in the 20 May 2013 issue of *Journal of Geophysical Research: Atmospheres*, these particulates are cooling the planet and, with as little as a 35% reduction in industrial activity, the global average temperature of Earth will skyrocket by 1 degree Celsius. Because this change will occur in about 6 weeks, far too rapidly for humans and most other complex organisms to keep pace, I cannot imagine we will long survive such an event. In other words, industrial activity constantly puts these "dimming" particulates into the atmosphere, most notably by burning coal high in sulfur. The particulates constantly fall out, very rapidly, while the GHG remain locked in blanket status and are constantly being added to as well. If we stop burning coal and other fossil fuels, the skies clear up, the GHG warm much more rapidly, and the global average temperature of Earth thus heats up far too quickly for adaptation.

Industrial civilization is a heat engine driving us to extinction. Turning off industrial civilization, or even reducing industrial activity by a relatively minor amount, causes loss of habitat for humans even faster than keeping industrial civilization running. Thus, the Catch-22 that has come to be known as the McPherson Paradox: With respect to industrial civilization, we are damned if we do, and we are damned if we don't.

The slow rise in planetary temperature to date has destroyed habitat for myriad species including, in many places, humans. The gradual rise in global average temperature since the beginning of the Industrial Revolution is proceeding 10,000 times faster than vertebrates can adapt, according to the stunningly conservative peer-reviewed journal *Literature*: specifically, a paper in the August, 2013 issue of *Ecology Letters* authored by Quintero and Wiens reached this dire conclusion. Yet abrupt climate change has begun only recently. An abrupt global-average rise in temperature resulting from the loss of global dimming taking Earth well above the 1750 baseline, with the vast majority of the temperature rise occurring within a few weeks or months, surely will destroy habitat for our species and many others far faster than expected. It is difficult for me to imagine much multicellular life on our only home with a rapid rise from the current temperature to a much warmer temperature even in a matter of decades, much less a few months.

## *Sixth Mass Extinction on Earth*

Item four is the ongoing Sixth Mass Extinction. The current rate of extinction of species, along with the current rise in planetary temperature, is unprecedented in planetary history.

Again, the ultra-conservative peer-reviewed journal *Literature* caught up to the Sixth Mass Extinction on June 19, 2015, with a paper in *Science Advances*. Coincident with the release of the paper, lead author Gerardo Ceballos concluded via interview, "Life would take many millions of years to recover, and our species itself would likely disappear early on." Indeed, a United Nations report issued during August, 2010 conservatively estimated the extinction rate of 150-200 species each day. Nearly five years later, the journal Literature caught up to the ongoing genocide.

Ceballos and colleagues penned a subsequent paper that appeared in the 25 July 2017 issue of *Proceedings of the National Academy of Sciences*. This paper is titled, "Biological Annihilation via the Ongoing Sixth Mass Extinction Signaled by Vertebrate Population Losses and Declines," and it reaches a far direr conclusion than the 2015 paper: "This 'biological annihilation' underlines the seriousness for humanity of Earth's ongoing sixth mass extinction event." In the final sentence, the paper concludes, "... painting a dismal picture of the future of life, including human life." The final nail in the planetary coffin appeared in *Scientific Reports* on 13 November 2018 with a paper titled, "Co-extinctions annihilate planetary life during extreme environmental change." The paper concludes that all life on Earth could disappear as a result of environmental stress associated with a rise in global average temperature of 5-6°C. Conservative analyses indicate Earth is headed for a higher temperature within the next few years, as demonstrated in future chapters.

The worst of the previous five Mass Extinction Events occurred about 252 million years ago. The "Great Dying" was characterized by a global-average rise in temperature from Ice Age -- 12 degrees C -- to hothouse and beyond: 23 degrees C (about 73°F). This is the warmest temperature experienced by Earth during the last 2 billion years. It has happened once in that time. According to my own conservative analysis in Chapter 3, we are headed for a similar temperature by mid-2026. That is in a very few years. I simply added up the primary contributors to global heating to come up with this result.

According to an analysis posted on the Arctic News blog on April 24, 2017, which assumes *exponential* temperature rise, rather than simply adding up the primary contributors of temperature rise, the planet will reach 23°C (about 73°F) -- some 9.5 degrees above the 1750 baseline -- in 2021. Lest you believe this is crazy, a similar analysis conducted in 2012 predicted only a global-average rise in temperature of 4°C above the 1750 baseline by 2030. The analysis from 2012 has proven wildly conservative.

Adding to the horrific news, Earth is also headed for an ice-free Arctic, as described in a paper written by Maslowski and colleagues that appeared in the 2012 issue of *Annual Review of Earth and Planetary Science.* This event last happened long before our species appeared on Earth. This 2012 paper predicted an ice-free Arctic in 2016, plus or minus three years. We have dodged six bullets so far, and it appears our luck is about to run out. An ice-free Arctic, which appears imminent in the very near future, seems likely to trigger the 50-Gt burst of methane ($CH_4$) from the relatively shallow seafloor of the Arctic Ocean described by field researcher Natalia Shakhova and colleagues at the European Geophysical Union meeting in 2008 as, "...highly possible for abrupt release at any time." Such an event would raise global-average temperature beyond the temperature experienced by humans in the past, and almost certainly would cause the demise of civilization as a result of our *inability to produce and store grains at large scale*, thereby adding even more warming due to the loss of global dimming as the aerosols fall to Earth.

People in bunkers might survive a few years. They will be dehydrated, hungry, lonely, and living within a bleak world nearly devoid of other complex life. Their survival will be a day-to-day proposition, with every day more tenuous than the day before, much as it is today for individuals of most non-human species.

## *After Coming to Grips with this Terminal Diagnosis, After Receiving and Truly Understanding this Direst of Situations, Then What?*

As item five, I would like to consider how we act. How do we integrate this knowledge into our lives? Who do we become?

I strongly suspect we are the final humans on Earth. In light of this knowledge, will you live more fully each day? Each moment? Will you become the best human you can imagine? Can you imagine *that?*

Will you prioritize your work differently? Or your relationships?

What is important to you? *Who* is important to you? Are you acting *now* as if these things and these beings are important?

Are you attached to the outcomes of your efforts? Or are you able to courageously and virtuously pursue justice, without a profound sense of disappointment when the universe does not bend to your will? Have you adopted, "let go, or be dragged," as one of the defining elements of your life?

Are you passionately pursuing a life of excellence? Or are you racing ever-faster on the treadmill on which you were born?

Are you able to define the meanings of your life? Are you pursuing what you love?

Are you doing what you love? Are you loving what you do? Are you doing it well?

## Peace on Earth

British philosopher Bertrand Russell wrote in 1950: "After ages during which the earth produced harmless trilobites and butterflies, evolution progressed to the point at which it generated Neros, Genghis Khans, and Hitlers. This, however, is a passing nightmare; in time the earth will become again incapable of supporting life, and peace will return."

Despite Russell's prescient words, every day I read about human hubris, rooted in civilization. We have convinced ourselves that we are stunningly special, as individuals, as members of industrial civilization, and as a species. We are special, at every level, as I have frequently pointed out. Considerably less impressive is how we have chosen to act toward the living planet, including other humans, with the unearned bounty handed us. Our individual and collective failures to recognize and alter our destructive ways have predictably led to our demise as individuals, as an industrial civilization, and as a species.

And yet we feign surprise -- or, worse yet, some people actually *are* surprised -- when individuals die, and when we learn about the near-term demise of our favorite civilization and our favorite species. The majority of the most horrifically reckless, self-absorbed animals in planetary history cannot accept the obvious outcome of its behavior. If only Bertrand Russell were here to comment.

The universe we inhabit is approximately 13.8 billion years old. Our species is about 300,000 years old. During a time exceeding considerably more than the initial 99% existence of the universe, *Homo sapiens* was not present. If the universe is all about us, as believed by people citing god(s), divine energy, "source" or various other imaginings, then the universe has been exceedingly patient.

This, of course, is all old news to thinking individuals. I am neither the first nor the wisest to tackle this issue: Social commentators were slogging through the lonely path of hip-deep mud for generations before I showed up, trying desperately to be heard and understood.

I might, however, be among the last individuals to write social commentary on Earth. Surely there will be a prize!

Principled words have been largely ignored. Principled actions have been largely disparaged. Small wonder the wisdom of our "sapient" species has been so brilliantly, cleverly disguised.

Industrial civilization teeters on the brink. Abrupt climate change is underway today. It is not a problem for the grandchildren. It is a predicament for today.

Any moment might be your last, as pointed out by Homer in *The Iliad.* As desert anarchist and social critic Edward Abbey pointed out, "Nirvana is now." Let us grab nirvana, one moment at a time.

Every day I am told by self-proclaimed friends that I ought not to make predictions. "Climate science is too complex," they say. As if Thales of Miletus did not receive the same criticism upon correctly predicting a solar eclipse in 585 BC. As if many people did not believe predictions of lunar and solar eclipses as recently as September of 2017. Science is predictive with far greater accuracy and precision than any other alternative.

Every day I am incorrectly assailed for encouraging inaction. These incorrect diagnoses come from people unable or unwilling to be fully present within the actual, physical universe. They are unaware of those I have influenced to live without fear or judgment. They are unwilling to embrace life, love, and the act of living fully. For these people I have given advice, in various outlets and various ways, most of it ignored and insulted.

I can lead a person to knowledge but I cannot make him think. I suspect my work as a teacher is done.

# The Crock-Pot of My Brain

Earth has experienced five mass extinction events, and we are in the midst of the Sixth. A mass extinction event occurs when at least 50 percent of all species on the planet disappear. Ultimately, everything goes extinct, including humans. Already half-a-dozen species in our own genus, the genus *Homo*, have gone extinct.

In April of 1896, Svente Arhenius wrote the first paper about global climate change published in the peer-reviewed journal *Literature*. In it, he predicted global warming would heat Earth 1°C due to the burning of fossil fuels as part of industrial civilization. He and his contemporaries thought that would be a great idea since a warmer Nordic region, they thought, would enable more food production and, of course, be more comfortable. Hardly anyone during the next 120 years imagined that warming could spell the extinction of our favorite species. We are looking at that happening soon. Not merely in our lifetimes, but within the next few years. We have entered the Sixth Mass Extinction, and our demise is on the menu. As the title of a recent peer-reviewed paper indicates, we are facing biological annihilation.

In 2002, while conducting research for a book I was co-editing, I came across evidence that led me to believe that habitat for human animals would soon be coming to an end due to abrupt planetary warming. This gave me pause: I realized the attendant inconvenience for humans. No habitat means no place to live. The information was so traumatic that I locked it away back in that dark little safe place in my head where I did not have to think about it. However, it was back there in the crock-pot of my mind, cooking...like Earth.

I was a busy man! I had students to teach, books to write, research to conduct, awards to win. Who has time to think about extinction? I was busy applying the Socratic method in my classrooms and also employing classroom anarchism, allowing my students to seize their learning rather than have me pour information down their not-so-hungry throats. I was entrenched in battling college deans and presidents who were tearing up native, desert gardens on the university campus to replace them with water fountains and a large grassy mall. In the desert! Putting a water-hungry feature on the campus of a university smack in the middle of the Sonoran Desert seemed insane to me. Pointing out the insanity did not endear me to university administrators rabidly in pursuit of money as a driver of economic growth. Virtually every administrator I encountered in more than 20 years as a professor could be described in a single line from renowned entrepreneur Peter Drucker: "A bad manager can take a good staff and destroy it, causing the best employees to flee and the remainder to lose all motivation."

After 18 years of teaching and receiving the highest academic awards at the university, I was relieved of teaching the classes in my home department. Now, this is very important: I was not fired, I was just not given any more classes to teach. I could collect my ivory-tower paycheck and stay at home, thank you very much. This was simultaneously the deepest insult and greatest reward a professor could receive. Especially a workaholic one like me who actually loved teaching and doing research.

Ironically, the resulting time off from classroom activities gave my crock-pot even more time to contemplate my early demise and the extinction of life on Earth. Even while participating in a social-justice project for incarcerated juveniles and adults called *Poetry Inside/Out*, I was busily researching the possible outcome of abrupt climate change on the planet's living organisms. It was not looking good for our big blue marble's passengers.

In 2007, I started to blog about our imminent extinction, peak oil, and the murderous culture of this industrial civilization that we inhabit. I came to believe that only the collapse of industrial civilization could save us from the life-punishing heat engine we recognize as civilization. And in a perfectly imperfect world, that would have been true. Except for two very important variables, that is, the first one had barely been studied by scientists and the second one I had not yet considered.

Meanwhile, the crock-pot in my brain was still stewing and I hatched a crazy plan to not only extend the life of my wife and myself but to serve as an example of right-action as I reduced my human footprint on the land. I cashed in my retirement accounts and created a platinum-grade, off-grid homestead in the desert of southern New Mexico. I then waited for everyone to follow me. Because. You know. Professor! White guy! Charming and entertaining! Who would not follow me into an off-grid lifestyle?

Crickets.

It was not long before I realized it was a good thing no one followed me.

What I had not calculated into the scenario more than a decade ago were the two most important variables associated with abrupt climate change resulting from industrial civilization.

One: global dimming. Two: the catastrophic meltdown of more than 450 nuclear reactors.

These two variables create the perfect storm of, "We are SOL and there is no turning back the clock."

Global dimming is the Catch-22 of global climate change. Greenhouse gases absorb solar radiation and warm the planet while aerosols, also being created every minute as a result of burning fossil fuels, reflect incoming solar radiation thus preventing the greenhouse gases from further warming Earth. Whereas greenhouse gases stay in the atmosphere for a long time, locking in the global-average temperature resulting from current $CO_2$ levels for at least a thousand years, these aerosols are constantly falling out of the atmosphere. So, it is actually easier to clean up the sky from pollution than it is to eliminate carbon dioxide and the dozens of other greenhouse gasses. This sounds great, but it also gives us quite the predicament: If we clean up our act, the aerosols fall out and we are cooked in a matter of weeks.

The second variable is the unprecedented and almost certain uncontrolled meltdown of more than 450 nuclear reactors due to the collapse of the heat engine known as civilization. It does not take a nuclear physicist to imagine that scenario. We have seen plenty of disaster movies, and we have seen it happen in real life at Chernobyl and Fukushima, two ongoing nuclear disasters. Imagine Fukushima times 100 and no people around to contain the meltdowns.

What does that look like? It looks like Earth's atmosphere being stripped away. It looks like Earth transitioning into a dead, Mars-like planet. It looks like never coming back from an extinction event, as the planet has the past five times.

And guess what? *no one* is working on either of those predicaments! At this late stage, they have become insoluble predicaments. Forty years ago, we might have had a chance. Twenty years ago, we may have had the possibility of a post-apocalyptic world to inhabit. Today, the chances of solving this predicament are bracketed by zero and none.

So, basically, the patient, Earth, is in stage four with days to live.

The crock-pot in my brain is just about boiling over at this point and I realize I am going to have to admit my own mortality is imminent. That, of course, is nothing new to me. Or to any of us. We all knew when we were kids that one day we were going to die, maybe we did not think it would be for a long time, but we knew it would happen. Eventually. Probably, like Svente Arhenius, we did not think we would be taking the planet with us into the abyss.

Or that there would be no one left to write dirges for us, or tell the story of how hard we fought to save our home and all Her lovely creatures.

When a patient is in stage four cancer with days to live, do the doctors keep telling her they are going to save her? That they could still invent a cure to turn back the clock? No, of course not. That would be lying. A doctor who is a decent human being will be honest and help set up hospice for the patient so she can be comfortable and have a chance to say goodbye to her loved ones in a safe space. In hospice, patients can complete their relationships and be made comfortable so they do not die in agonizing pain or loneliness or filled with the false hope of a miracle cure that is never coming. Stephen Jenkinson has done a great deal of work in this area and it would be worth anyone's time to read his books and listen to his interviews.

Back to global dimming and 450+ nuclear reactors. That is when I realized my crock-pot was done and I fully embraced the terrifying reality of our situation, in all its tragic beauty.

We are going extinct, and soon. The only way to walk into this strange and alien future is with the analogy of being in hospice. Every one of us. Together.

Can we imagine nearly 8 billion people saying goodbye to each other in hospice? No longer worrying about our careers, or reputations, or mortgages, or where we will get our water from, or warlords, or pandemics, or the truly mundane parts of life like doing dishes and taking out the trash and doing laundry, which in the end seem bittersweet.

On a person's deathbed, they are either alone or surrounded by those they love, and they are not thinking about anything else except the people who meant something to them during their life.

Because at the edge of extinction, only love remains.

# Chapter 2: The Politics and Science of Our Demise

*Extinction is the rule. Survival is the exception.*

(Carl Sagan)

Very few mainstream scientists could speak or write about near-term human extinction and remain supported in their jobs. Therefore, very few do. Very few go the distance in connecting the dots regarding our imminent demise. Paradoxically, tenure is designed to protect academic freedom. Administrators walk a tightrope as they promote the insanity of the dominant paradigm in the name of money while simultaneously paying lip service to academic freedom.

I will make it personal, while quoting Elisabeth Kübler-Ross from her famous book, *On Death and Dying*: "Those patients who were told of their fatal diagnosis without a chance, without a sense of hope, reacted the worst and never quite reconciled themselves with the person who presented the news to them in this cruel manner." In the latter pages of her 1969 book, Kübler-Ross warned the reader not to steal hope from his or her audience. The outcome for me, as I selflessly ignored her advice: Most of the people previously part of my life have failed to reconcile themselves with the person who presented the dire news to them in an honest manner (a manner Kübler-Ross would undoubtedly call cruel, thus promoting ignorance in the name of bliss).

As with my personal life, I took a radical approach in my classrooms for a very long time. In return, my final department head was hired specifically to make my life miserable enough that I would leave. After all, it is nearly impossible to fire a tenured full professor with the record I had established. However, I did leave active service voluntarily because I was unwilling to continue my participation in an irredeemably corrupt system. It was a system so sick that it drove away someone who actually loved being in the classroom, a rarity in the university world.

The evidence I present is conservative and accurate, in this book and throughout my life. The conservatism and accuracy are not dependent upon who uncovers the evidence. The following analysis is based on Sam Carana's assessment in the *Arctic News Blog* from 15 July 2016. Carana is probably at least two anonymous people with unknown credentials. I suspect Carana is two or three climate scientists who would like to retain their academic or government positions. In other words, I suspect they are avoiding the mistake I made by presenting evidence under their own names within celebrity culture. Carana makes mistakes, like everybody else, but these errors do not obviate "his/her" assessment from July, 2016.

Carana's analysis is good. S/he is able and willing to connect a few dots within the arena of abrupt climate change. The resulting analysis is generally quite conservative, although I believe s/he errs on the side of overheating once or twice. In the first case, s/he concludes global-average temperature has increased by 1.92°C since 1750. Although a paper by Mark Richardson and colleagues published in the 27 June 2016 online issue of *Nature Climate Change* indicates direct observations have missed about 19% of global warming since the 1860s. I will low-ball the scientific consensus in going with 1.7°C so far. The second error, mentioned below, is more substantive.

Tacking onto the current temperature the amount of global warming locked in for the next decade adds 0.5°C to the current temperature of Earth. From my conservative point of view, that takes us to 2.2°C above baseline (i.e., about 1750).

Removal of the aerosol masking effect, or global dimming, adds an additional 2.5°C. This rise in temperature is guaranteed by high, unstable temperatures that preclude large-scale production of grains. The very conservative journal *Literature* concludes the resultant heating will be up to about 3°C, but I will take the ultra-conservative approach and side with Carana on this one.

Albedo changes in the Arctic, in light of rapidly diminishing ice, add 1.6°C to the total. This addition results from Peter Wadhams's work in 2012 concluding that energy absorption will increase by more than 2 Watts per square meter. But absorption has already increased from 0.43 Watts per square meter during the period between 1970 and 1992 to 0.75 Watts per square meter since 1992. A near-term ice-free Arctic thus increases the global-average temperature by 1.6°C in the next ten years.

According to Carana's analysis, seafloor methane adds only 1.1°C between now and 2026 (about 2°F). This figure is stunningly conservative relative to predictions by field researchers Natalia Shakhova and colleagues. They conclude a 50-gigatonne burst of methane is "...highly possible for abrupt release at any time." Therefore, I will use the conservative figure of 1.1°C.

Carana adds 2.1°C for extra water-vapor feedback. In doing so, s/he is concluding that essentially all the rise in temperature between 1750 and 2016 is owing to carbon dioxide and will be matched by a similar rise in temperature in the near future because of water vapor. A more conservative approach pins the carbon dioxide contribution to 0.85°C, and therefore reduces the water-vapor feedback to 0.85°C. There will be an additional 0.5°C added in a decade, as indicated above. Thus, I will subtract 0.85°C from Carana's projected water-vapor contribution.

Finally, Carana adds 0.3°C for other feedbacks. Considering the latest information about terrestrial permafrost and more than five dozen other self-reinforcing feedback loops, this figure seems startlingly conservative. Therefore, I use it here.

Habitat for humans on Earth is rapidly diminishing. Wishful thinking aside, cleverness aside, self-proclaimed intelligence aside, human animals will not persist long without habitat. Abrupt climate change has barely begun and the Sixth Mass Extinction is clearly underway. Afflicted by the arrogance of humanism, many members of my species believe the concept of habitat is applicable to other species, but not ours.

In total, Carana ends up with 10.02°C above baseline by mid-2026, which is about 23.5°C global-average temperature. *That would be the highest global-average temperature on this planet during the last 2,000,000,000 years.* Taking a conservative approach at every step, I conclude there will "only" be an 8.95°C rise in temperature by mid-2026. As a result, I conclude global-average temperature at that time will be about 22.45°C (13.5°C + 8.95°C). This is notably above 22°C, the temperature at which Earth has most commonly found itself during the last 2,000,000,000 years. I suspect it is more likely, based on the conservative journal *Literature*, that Earth will hit 23°C or more in mid-2026. There is no reason to expect Earth to start cooling until dozens of self-reinforcing feedback loops are inexplicably reversed.

For context, the Great Dying wiped out nearly all complex life on Earth. It involved a global-average rise in temperature from about 12°C to about 23°C (about 54°F to about 73°F) during a span of several hundred or a few tens of thousands of years. To conclude that humans will survive a similar rise in temperature within only a couple of hundred years, with the vast majority of the heating occurring within a decade, is exceedingly -- and probably insanely -- optimistic. Considering *Homo sapiens* is strongly dependent upon myriad other species for our own survival, it is difficult to imagine our favorite species will have the habitat requisite for survival as we barrel into 2026, only a few years from now.

As my partner, Pauline Schneider, writes about our human fragility, "We are a soft-skinned, naked animal. We have no fur, no scales, no claws, no fangs or poisons. We depend upon easily found food, housing, community, clean water (bad water is still the leading cause of human death globally) to survive the week. We have been outlived by dragonflies, butterflies, alligators, and sharks by tens and even hundreds of millions of years. Six previous incarnations of our genus are extinct in short order and yet we are arrogant enough to think we can survive without habitat and alone."

But perhaps we will survive. Perhaps the heat engine known as civilization will be repaired by soon-to-be-developed "tools that cool" that will be created -- of course -- via the heat engine known as civilization. Perhaps we can bomb the deserts and roam the ocean in nuclear submarines while eating "Soylent Green." Then, a few million years later, assuming the planet cools, perhaps we will pop out the other side of a substantial bottleneck in sufficient numbers to do it all over again. Between now and then, I fully expect 10,000 trolls will emerge from beneath 10,000 bridges to claim I am an extremist making up the notion of near-term human extinction as a means of generating income for myself.

Unicorns and other miracles notwithstanding, our persistence would surprise me. I am preternaturally inclined toward reality instead of wishful thinking.

Perhaps that is one of my problems: I simply do not wish hard enough.

## Faster than Expected

As indicated above, I doubt there will be a human on Earth by 2026. Indeed, I doubt there will be a significant amount of complex life on this planet by then. It will be a small world, as was the case in the wake of each of the five prior Mass Extinction events on Earth. Bacteria, fungi, and microbes will dominate.

Humans will lose habitat on Earth before the last human dies. The final human probably will die after running out of canned food or potable water in a bunker. He or she may not even know human extinction has occurred.

The ice-free Arctic projected to occur in 2016 $\pm 3$ years by Maslowski and colleagues in their 2012 paper seems likely in 2019 or 2020. As President Niinisto of Finland pointed out in a White House Joint Press Conference with U.S. President Trump on 28 August 2017: "The problem is not only Arctic; if we lose the Arctic, we lose the globe. That is the reality."

President Niinistö was referring to the tremendous burst of planetary warming certain to occur in the wake of an ice-free Arctic Ocean. Not only would absorption further outstrip reflectance due to the reduction in albedo, but methane would spew even faster out of the Arctic and into the atmosphere. Methane, in the short term, is more than 100 times more potent than carbon dioxide as a greenhouse gas.

Arctic ice is very fragile going into the 2018 melt season. Regardless when it arrives, the near-term, ice-free Arctic will be experienced by *Homo sapiens* for the first time. This event might trigger the 50-Gt burst of methane forecast by Shakhova and colleagues at the European Geophysical Union annual meeting in 2008 ("We consider the release of up to 50 Gt of predicted amount of hydrate storage as highly possible for abrupt release at any time"). The findings of Shakhova and colleagues were reinforced by a paper they published in the 22 June 2017 online issue of *Nature Communications* illustrating the mechanisms for abrupt destabilization of methane clathrates. Further support came from a paper by Serov and colleagues in the 3 October 2017 issue of *Proceedings of the National Academy of Sciences*. I reasonably use the ice-free Arctic as a proxy for this first burst of atmospheric methane. After all, it has been "highly possible for abrupt release at any time" for more than a decade.

The first 50-gigatonne burst of methane described by Shakhova et al. translates to a global temperature rise of more than 1°C (about 1.8°F), within a matter of months. This abrupt rise in temperature would heat Earth beyond the point of habitation by our species and it would undoubtedly cause civilization to collapse because grains no longer could be grown on a large scale. Industrial civilization, as with its predecessors, requires grain production, storage, and distribution. This abrupt rise in temperature would be felt within a few weeks in the Northern Hemisphere -- where nearly all civilization-supporting grains are grown -- and within a year throughout the world. The rate of change would preclude adaptation by humans and most other animals.

Lack of global dimming adds at least another 2.5°C (about 4.4°F). Earth is then nearly 6°C (about 11°F) above the 1750 baseline by the following spring (2020/2021?). About 2/3 of the temperature rise comes within a few months. I doubt there will be habitat for humans or many other animals at that point. After all, the slow rise in global-average temperature documented through 2012 has outstripped the ability of vertebrates to adapt by more than 10,000 times, according to a paper by Quintero and Wiens published in the August, 2013 issue of *Ecology Letters*. Mammals cannot keep up either, as indicated by a 15 October 2018 paper by Matt Davis and colleagues in the *Proceedings of the National Academy of Sciences*.

Humans are vertebrates. Humans are mammals. Neither vertebrates nor mammals can keep pace with the ongoing Sixth Mass Extinction.

In other words, not long after civilization fails -- and almost certainly by 2026 -- the planet will harbor no humans. Not in bunkers. Not in caves, eating canned peaches. I will go well beyond betting my life on it: I will bet human existence.

Some claim Earth's climate sensitivity is insufficient to permit a global-average rise in temperature with such rapidity. They claim the oceans will buffer the Southern Hemisphere, which has relatively little land surface. They claim there would be a long lag between a volcanic ejection and the subsequent change in global dimming. In making these claims, they are ignorant of the evidence: Climate sensitivity is exceptionally high, as pointed out by numerous recent articles in the peer-reviewed journal *Literature*.

In the extremely unlikely event there is a human on Earth in a few years, that person will be hungry, thirsty, lonely, and bathing in ionizing radiation. Every day will be more tenuous than the day before, as is already the case for most organisms on this planet. Habitat for human animals might return in a few million years. Humans will not. Extinction is forever.

Some people are preparing for the collapse of civilization. I used to be one of them. Now I spend my days living, rather than pursuing dying more slowly than others.

It is not as if I *desire* near-term human extinction via abrupt climate change or by any other means. I do know all species go extinct, even the ones we love. Unfortunately, I am capable of connecting the few dots that lead directly, irrevocably to our demise. Contrary to the vast majority of people I know, I am not afraid of the truth, even though it involves my death in the very near future.

And, to be clear, I did not cause near-term human extinction as a result of abrupt climate change. It was not even my idea! Nobody accuses the plumber of causing a plugged water line.

I doubt my radicalism gives way to wishful thinking. I doubt my love of life on Earth dissipates and fades away until I meet my untimely demise.

*Carpe diem* (seize the day). There aren't many of them left.

*Pressum Diem* (squeeze the day). Make every one matter. Like all of us, the days are going away faster than expected.

## Predicaments Lack Solutions

Aldo Leopold wrote, in his 1949 book *A Sand County Almanac*: "One of the penalties of an ecological education is that one lives alone in a world of wounds. Much of the damage inflicted on land is quite invisible to laymen. An ecologist must either harden his shell and make believe that the consequences of science are none of his business, or he must be the doctor who sees the marks of death in a community that believes itself well and does not want to be told otherwise."

As "...the doctor who sees the marks of death in a community that believes itself well and does not want to be told otherwise," I am fed up with ridiculous "solutions." Climate change is an insoluble predicament, not merely a problem. If there were a solution, I believe the people pulling the levers of industry would know about it. I do not believe they enjoy the prospect of human extinction.

Civilization is responsible for life-destroying, abrupt climate change. Turning off civilization kills us all faster. If this seems like a Catch-22, then you have it figured out.

I am not suggesting that correctly identifying the predicament leads to a solution. It does not. Predicaments sometimes have no solutions.

I promote and practice a gift economy and, with very few exceptions, it is a one-way street. To employ the language of American writer Daniel Quinn, takers outnumber leavers. This is among the many reasons I no longer expect better from humans, even those I know well. Civilization will kill us all, and it has already destroyed the ethical character of most people I have known. As a result, people generally believe what they want to believe, evidence notwithstanding.

Principled actions are the bane of civilization. No bad deed goes unrewarded.

We are all products of our genetics and our personal history. These attributes tend to dictate who we are, but they need not limit us. I appreciate, although I can never fully understand, that some people have experienced abuse or other horrors. Those horrors need not come up in every conversation to explain contemporary shortcomings. Many adults, abused as children, share with graduates of the University of California at Berkeley and evangelical vegans the need to share their experience with everybody they meet, typically within the first 10 minutes. I understand and appreciate our near-absence of free will. In addition, I understand better than most people the shackles of imperialism.

There are still things I do not understand. In addition, apparently, there remain a few people I have yet to offend. Ergo, this chapter, which includes a few examples from among many.

Politics remains my favorite brand of lunacy. The supporter of any party or politician remains my favorite brand of lunatic. To believe we can rely on politics to solve an insoluble predicament created by the life-destroying heat engine of civilization is bizarre. Politicians transfer money, typically from people who have little money to people who have a lot of it, while blaming others. Believing your favorite politician will address any of your concerns is naively cute. The system is not broken, it is fixed. However, it is not fixed for you or me. Or Planet Earth!

The proselytizing vegan remains high on my list of misguided "fix-it" solutionistas. Living in the world of should, rather than reality, religious acolytes of veganism first try to convince me a planetary change in human diets will prevent runaway climate change. They say it will save us. When I point out it is too late for that, they change course. Now, they say, veganism will save *me*. I'm fine, thanks. Please keep your salvation to yourself.

Veganism, sometimes called "a way of being" by true believers, is no solution at any level. Claiming compassion via dietary preference -- although many vegans go beyond the realm of dietary preference and into the realm of religion -- is delusional when the diet is vegan. Delusion is exactly what I have come to expect from a dumbed-down, willfully ignorant populace. Particularly galling is the inability to understand the extreme environmental cost of veganism.

There is no free lunch. Moving down the food web *shifts* the impact rather than reducing it. Eating a diet rich in soy, grains, fruits, and nuts increases and exacerbates agricultural intensification. The example of genetically modified soy destroying essentially every terrestrial form of life on Earth is not sufficiently convincing to the typical proselytizing vegan. California's Central Valley milked dry for almonds is not sufficiently convincing to the typical proselytizing vegan. Among the other costs obvious to ecologists and ignored by proselytizing vegans: organisms that depend upon the rapidly vanishing grasslands and savannas of the world. Apparently, no evidence is sufficiently convincing to true believers of veganism.

The typical proselytizing vegan will claim she does not eat many grains, the large-scale production and distribution of which are fundamental to propping up civilization. Such a self-absorbed response makes approximately as much sense as the notion that my walking away from imperialism will terminate imperialism. I did. It did not. The proselytizing vegan could learn from my failure. Yet I doubt she will.

Veganism is the flip side of eating flesh for every meal. At least the meat-eaters know what they are killing: It's on the plate. Vegans deny their murderous diets are nevertheless responsible for the damage. After all, ignorance of the crime being committed is no defense. Using a dietary preference to maintain the omnicidal heat engine of civilization is disingenuous at best. Do not even get me started on the polluted ocean resulting from a vegan diet.

Holistic Resource Management offered by snake-oil salesman Allan Savory is yet another faux solution lapped up by the ignorant masses. I have been pointing out Savory's silliness since my days as a researcher in graduate school. I filed an overview on my blog in March, 2013.

I am fed up with magical thinking, too. They -- whoever *they* are -- are not trying to kill us with "chemtrails." If they are trying to kill us with chemtrails -- and they are not -- then they are failing badly. We add more than 200,000 people to the planet every day, births minus deaths. If they are trying to positively influence the weather with chemtrails -- and they are not -- then they are failing badly.

Killing us is easy: War has worked nicely at every point in history. Civilized humans fall for that trick every time. We are easy to goad into hating an "other." Any "other" will do, for most of us, most of the time. No "chemtrails" needed.

Enough with the books, too. I do not doubt your book has all the answers, but I do not have time to review it before it is published. I do not have time to read it after it is published either. I simply do not have time. I side with author and teacher Jack Kornfield on this one with a line frequently but incorrectly attributed to the Buddha: "The trouble is, you think there's time."

All of the above applies to your film, too. Also, your workshop, your philosophy, your favorite brand of meditation, your hemp, and, for that matter, every conceivable combination of every imaginable "solution."

I have actually pondered my place in the universe. I do not doubt your sincerity, but I sincerely doubt you can put much of a dent in my worldview. You are a few decades too late for that.

I need to be clear about this: I really do not mind your dietary choices, your politics, or your perspective on any topic. I just do not want your perspective pushed into my world. Jehovah's Witnesses are welcome in my world. Proselyting Jehovah's Witnesses are not welcome. Ditto for anybody else proselyting about anything else.

I remain open to new information, as long as it is grounded in reality. If your proposed "solution" violates the Laws of Thermodynamics, please make sure it is approved by the U.S. Patent Office before you send it my way.

## Mangling My Message

I am often accused of encouraging people who follow my work to pursue hedonism. Alternatively, I am occasionally accused of causing the suicide of somebody who read my writing or heard me speak. There seems no middle ground. Here I will start with a definition and a line from gonzo journalist Hunter S. Thompson, respectively.

Hedonism, according to the definitions in my dictionary, include (1) the doctrine that pleasure or happiness is the sole or chief good in life, and (2) a way of life that is based on or suggesting the principles of hedonism. Consistent with the notion of hedonism, Thompson is renowned for his line, "I hate to advocate drugs, alcohol, violence, or insanity to anyone, but they've always worked for me."

Please do not misinterpret me. I am hardly a prude. I am a huge fan of pleasure. Of course, I have no problem with happiness, as long as it is not confused with joy or acquisition of material possessions. Hedonism seems a few materialistic steps beyond pleasure, perhaps into the realm of ecstasy. As with everybody I know, I love feeling ecstatic.

The issue is clearly one of degree. I suspect we enter difficult ethical terrain when pleasure becomes *the sole or chief good in life.* Defining moderation, as sought by Socrates, is a worthy pursuit (ditto for the remaining handful of Socrates' pursuits, namely justice, good, virtue, piety, and courage). The ancient expression, "nothing too much" -- unfortunately twisted into the contemporary phrase, "moderation in all things," -- has great merit.

My standard response to the accusation that my message leads people down the path of hedonism is to ask when hedonism has been recently forsaken in the country of my birth? Most members of the privileged audience believe I am joking. A short time later, we turn out the lights and the people in the audience drive home, stopping only for a quick bite to eat in one of the restaurants they pass on the way to their two-car garage in suburbia.

When did irony die? Did I miss the celebration of life, which used to be called a funeral?

Most people claim, contrary to Hunter S. Thompson's quote, that they detest violence. Yet these same people benefit from, and apparently appreciate, the oppression and early deaths of people who happen to live in the vicinity of fossil fuels requisite to maintenance of American Empire, also known as "keeping the lights on."

A line from long-dead American comedian Bill Hicks is apropos: "There are essentially only two drugs that Western civilization tolerates: Caffeine from Monday to Friday to energize you enough to make you a productive member of society, and alcohol from Friday to Monday to keep you too stupid to figure out the prison that you are living in." These are the drugs Thompson claimed he appreciated, in his clever, insightful manner. I suspect he agreed with Hicks, although we will probably never know because Hicks and Thompson are both dead.

So much for violence and drugs. What about insanity?

What more can be said about a culture gone mad? Thousands of volumes have described individual and societal madness within the culture of contemporary, industrial civilization. I have predicted an acceleration of violence for more than two decades as economic contraction proceeds. Yet the mad march on, believing themselves sane because their indoctrination is so stunningly complete.

There is no external escape. There is no place to hide. Only by introspection can one escape the madness of contemporary culture.

No drugs needed. You can skip the alcohol, violence, and insanity, too.

## *Your Magic Number*

Every mentally well person older than 12 years of age -- insert your own joke here -- knows that everybody dies. Yet essentially everybody acts as if the concept of death applies only to non-human animals and also to other people. Rather than living with death in mind, thus with urgency, we occasionally take an online longevity quiz to comfort ourselves and then keep living as if we will make it comfortably to the century mark.

A similar mentality afflicts societal endeavors. Among the best known from the corporate media are the climate-change projections indicating all is well until 2100. After that, look out!

Once you admit and accept your own death, life takes on new meaning. Various activities become less worthy of one's time. Relationships rise in importance as the acquisition of fiat currency declines in priority.

And that is all childish and ethereal relative to the urgency of life in hospice. Admitting one's death in a century, or even in a decade, is one thing. Admitting one's death in three days is quite another.

What is *your* magic number? At what point will you live differently in light of your terminal diagnosis? Do you want to receive the "bad news" six months in advance? Six weeks? Six days? Six hours? Six minutes? Or perhaps not at all?

At some point, does it become irrelevant to you? Is it better for the medical doctor to lie to you? If so, at what point is it acceptable for the doctor to lie? Six months in advance? Six weeks? Six days? Six hours? Six minutes? Or perhaps it is always better for the medical doctor to play god.

What is *your* magic number?

I do not know your expiration date. Neither do you. If I had to guess, I would guess my guess is better than yours. It is sooner, too. Almost everybody reading these words has a remaining lifespan of weeks or months, not years. Decades? Fuhgedabahit!

I am not pleased with this prognosis. The results of my latest online longevity quiz indicate I have decades to go. So does the latest assessment from the Intergovernmental Panel on Climate Change (IPCC). The online quiz is the more reliable source of the two. It is still wrong because it fails to account for abrupt climate change, hence a lack of habitat for humans on Earth.

The overwhelmingly adverse response I have received to my message suggests many people are misinterpreting my intent. I am not calling for world peace with sociopaths at the helm. I am a tad more pragmatic than that. Please allow me to reiterate and elucidate below.

## *You are going to die. So is everybody else. Both will occur faster than expected.*

Surely this is not a surprise. Surely you did not believe our species could foul its own nest for thousands of years without adverse consequences.

Or maybe you bought into the infinite-growth paradigm. Bummer for you. Bummer for us.

## *Remain calm. Nothing is under control.*

Not by you. Not by me.

I have tried shouting from the rooftops. I have described the horrors of abrupt climate change since my earliest essays on the topic more than a decade ago. Shouting did not work for me. I doubt it will work for you. Everybody who wants to know about abrupt climate change surely knows by now. If somebody wants to know and does not know, more shouting is not likely to help.

Ergo, remain calm even as the ship takes on water. Death with dignity might even calm a few people around you as they reach the end.

There is an exception: We all influence, and perhaps even control, the emotions of a few people near us. Do you want to be an asshole with those people? Knock yourself out. You must be among the trolls who seek my errors. This slim volume is not for you.

## Pursue Excellence

As I have indicated a few dozen times, I am not interested in defining this simple statement. I can point you to a dictionary. I suspect you are familiar with examples from your own life.

I have indicated the lack of recognition, much less reward, of pursuing excellence in a culture of mediocrity. I have written and said there are only internal, personal rewards for pursuing excellence, notably the ability to look oneself in the mirror without remorse, shame, or guilt.

You want more? Of course, you do. The culture demands more, and virtually everyone reading these words is afflicted with cultural norms. I further articulate the benefits of pursuing excellence.

## Pursue Love

I am not interested in defining the pursuit of love. Again, I could point you to a dictionary. I could give examples, but there is no need to bother. After all, you already know.

I have indicated the lack of recognition, much less reward, of pursuing love in a culture of indifference. I have repeatedly written and said there are only internal, personal rewards for pursuing love and doing what you love, notably the ability to look oneself in the mirror, as I said above, without remorse, shame, or guilt.

You want more? Of course, you do. The culture demands more, and virtually everyone reading these words is afflicted with cultural norms. Below I further articulate the benefits of pursuing love.

## But What Shall I do?

This is the question to which I respond daily to people I barely know. I expand beyond the definitions of excellence and love. I invoke Buddhist-inspired right action rooted in the alleviation of suffering. I promote a lack of attachment to outcomes. Still, the question persists: *What shall I do?*

Do what is right. Do what you love. Do it well.

After all that, still the question persists. In the few paragraphs that follow, I take a turn for the pragmatic. Let the character assassination begin. Trust me: It is nothing new.

I am driven to a life of service. I do not know why. Perhaps you are similarly motivated. If so, good for the world. Too bad for you, though.

To me, for me, a life of service is everything. I could no more pursue fiat currency for the sake of having more prestige, power, or position than I could weasel my way into a tenured faculty position at a major research university. Not with my calm and calming messages of the pursuit of excellence and love. Not within a culture of mediocrity and indifference.

Perhaps service beyond your own life is important to you. If so, you might be interested in providing the means by which people can be alleviated of their suffering. You might be interested in the notions of hospice or, as Stephen Jenkinson calls it, the "death trade." You might be interested in "dying wisely," to again quote Jenkinson. You might be interested in helping others do the same. If so, then you have options.

You can become educated in hospice. Perhaps of more immediate concern, you can pursue knowledge about the likely causes of death in your area. Where I lived for 27 months in the Maya Mountains of western Belize, I suspect dehydration, physiological breakdown of the body's ability to cool itself, starvation, and suicide will be the leading causes of human mortality, in descending order. As a consequence, I studied symptoms of those afflictions and I encouraged others around me to do the same. I will use these causes of death as examples throughout the remainder of this chapter.

I invoke American ecologist Garrett Hardin's oft-asked question, "And then what?" Once my nearby acquaintances and I are sufficiently skilled to recognize symptoms, then what is next?

Obviously, alleviating suffering is key. Alleviating dehydration is relatively easy if water is accessible. If it is not -- and it will not be for millions of city-dwellers in the near future -- then alleviating mental and emotional suffering will be key as humans die before our eyes. I suspect the ability to remain calm will be important.

To alleviate the pain and potential mortality associated with

the physiological breakdown of the body's ability to cool itself is no small endeavor. A temperature of 35°C (95°F) at 100% relative humidity is likely to be lethal after just a few hours due to organ failure. Lethality can also result from a combination of higher temperature with lower relative humidity. And simply blowing air across a dying companion will not work under these circumstances. Instead, cool water must be applied.

Although we planned for this contingency, there was no guarantee such water would be available. At this point, and for millions of people around the globe in the near future, alleviating mental and emotional suffering will be key as humans die before our eyes. And I repeat: I suspect the ability to remain calm will be important.

Starvation is easy to deal with only when food is available. Those days are nearly behind all of us. As climate change accelerates into the future, food will be lacking for every person on Earth. We can store food, as I did for several years at the mud hut in New Mexico (it is still there). Stored food ultimately turns bad or becomes depleted. The near-term inability to grow food because habitat for complex life disappears from Earth indicates storage is a short-term solution to a long-term problem. Nuclear submarines and the International Space Station are relevant models. Alleviating mental and emotional suffering for ourselves and others will be key as humans starve to death before our eyes. And I say once again: I suspect the ability to remain calm will be important as this ongoing, accelerating disaster plays out.

Finally, there is the issue of suicide. It is one of many taboo topics in this culture. As I have indicated for a few years with a permalink post near the top of the page at my blog, guymcpherson.com, I am not afraid to take on this particular "taboo" topic. Rather, I advocate for a reasoned approach.

Every human has the right, albeit not legally in many places, to terminate his or her own life. Such an act can be thoughtful. I am personally non-judgmental toward people who choose an early exit. To be clear, I will repeat myself: *Such an act can be thoughtful.* I encourage thoughtful actions of all kinds. I am generally ignored or insulted in response. If you are intent upon taking the Hemingway out, please consider those you are leaving behind.

Perhaps the most thoughtful approach to suicide I have seen documented was taken by Martin Manley. He committed suicide on his sixtieth birthday, 15 August 2013. Before doing so, he created a weblog describing in considerable detail why he did so: http://martin-manley.eprci.com/. Even for those who are not considering suicide, Manley's extensive writing on the topic is worth reading.

# Chapter 3: Living with Urgency

*The meaning of life is to find your gift. The purpose of life is to give it away.*

(Pablo Picasso)

Consistent with the line from Picasso, I have found my gift. I am continuing to give it away, to the benefit of all concerned. I encourage the passionate pursuit of excellence and love, with an eye on urgency.

I have learned a lot since I voluntarily left active service as a tenured professor at a major university, the University of Arizona. I was 49 years old when I cut the monetary cord in May of 2009. Perhaps by sharing some of this knowledge, I can continue to encourage learning, creativity, and pushing beyond the shackles of culture into which we were born.

My goal in leaving active service from the privileged life of the academy was to lead by example. I wanted to prevent Earth from experiencing abrupt, irreversible climate change, the Sixth Mass Extinction, and other adverse outcomes caused by civilization. I failed in this most important of endeavors. I was probably at least two decades late getting started, and opting out of industrial civilization proved troublesome on several fronts.

Most importantly, however, despite my decision, I continued to teach. Nearly as important, I continued to learn. The 2.7-acre homestead in the wilds of southern, rural New Mexico provided many teachable moments for me and my hundreds of visitors. So, too, did the 57-acre homestead I occupied in western Belize.

At the homestead I called the mud hut in southern, rural New Mexico, I learned how to grow food. I learned how to design and build structures. I learned animal husbandry. I built structures to house non-human animals. I learned how to milk goats. I became adept, even expert, at making Mozzarella, Feta, and Parmesan. Once I even made something closely resembling blue cheese, which would have been more impressive had I not been trying to make Monterey Jack.

I learned that attempting to live beyond the dominant, patriarchal paradigm will be punished. Such action is met with confusion, disdain, and hatred, all rooted in ignorance.

According to most people, there is one way to live. Anything else is a mistake. Based on the reactions I have received, merely attempting to live beyond the mainstream may well be a mistake.

I learned a lot about human behavior, and most of what I learned contradicted my prior idealism. I learned most people are neither particularly intelligent nor capable of critical thinking. They believe cultural lies without question. They believe what they want to believe, contrary to the evidence. They promulgate lies without regard to evidence or the ensuing harm.

In other words, I learned that most people cannot be trusted. I learned most people are takers. Yet I still refuse to sacrifice love for cynicism, which would be among the greatest mistakes a person could make.

I learned a little kindness goes a long way. I learned we can all use more kindness and less judgment for the benefit of all. As nearly as I can tell, very few people have learned any of these simple concepts. It is no wonder, at least to me, that we are headed for human extinction very soon.

Most people, including at least 95% of the people I know, will gladly give away human habitat in exchange for a few fancy bills colored with ink. It is, therefore, small wonder the looming ice-free Arctic spells the demise of habitat for humans on Earth.

*Homo sapiens* has conquered the globe, for now. But, as we will all soon learn, nature bats last.

During the intervening time between now and my near-term expiration date, I intend to live fully, with intention. I will continue to pursue rationalism, too. It will no doubt continue to be a lonely path fraught with insults. However, I would rather be alone than unprincipled. Please join me, and the slim minority, along a principled path.

Adhering to principle and accepting human extinction need not induce despair. Unlike most of my many detractors, I am not miserable. Indeed, the ability to face the mirror without shame is a pleasant experience.

I smile and laugh frequently every day. Absurdism, the unintentionally hilarious actions of my detractors, and the presence of supportive friends combine to bring me joy. May your final days be equally fine.

## *Looking Back*

More than a decade ago, I believed I could foster change. Inspired to save humanity, my quest for a "sustainable path" *temporarily* overwhelmed my inner teacher. I sought to become one of the ten percent of the human population required to grow food for the rest of the populace on the homestead I created in New Mexico. I succeeded in my quest. Initially barely able to distinguish a screwdriver from a zucchini, I was growing sufficient food to feed many people by my second year in the garden.

Success is not what it used to be. Now I understand the notion of global dimming.

I believed a few others would change along with me. I overestimated the people nearest me.

I believed the masses would be willing to change if only to save habitat for their children. How hilarious is that?

My audiences and platforms have changed markedly since my days on campus. Then, the bond I forged with students from my classrooms encompassed every part of their lives and lasted decades. Now, the connection tends to be more fleeting.

Barefoot College at the mud hut in New Mexico represented a transition from the classrooms and coffee shops of Tucson, Berkeley, College Station, Grinnell, Moscow, Ames, and Cedar City, Utah to presentation halls throughout the world and the homestead I occupied briefly in western Belize. I hosted hundreds of people at the mud hut in New Mexico who were interested in homesteading, including a couple of dozen willing to work a few hours daily in exchange for the acquired knowledge, along with room and board. If they were to be believed, many lives were changed.

Many of the guests in Belize were seeking a cultural exchange. As a result, in some ways, they resembled the students from my days on campus and also my visitors at the homestead in New Mexico. They were usually young, intellectually curious, and willing to question the dominant narrative echoing through their heads. They were seeking independence, yet they were willing to work and learn alongside their contemporaries. Again, if they were to be believed, many lives were changed in Belize as well. Some were changed in the direction of kindness.

The usual response to my suggestion of kindness: "Why?"

My retort: "Why not?"

The conversation continues: "Yeah, but if we only have a few years left, why be kind?"

Does a terminal diagnosis preclude decency? Respect? Kindness?

Does hospice mean abandoning values? Does it translate to hedonism?

Does the fact that birth is a terminal illness that has proven fatal in every case mean we need to act as if our actions do not matter? Does acknowledging death preclude living with integrity?

I ask myself at least a dozen times daily whether my actions match my purpose. Am I pursuing excellence? Am I doing what I love? Am I doing it well? Am I acting respectfully, lovingly, to those around me?

In addition, I ask whether I am remaining true to my scientific side. After all, every legitimate scientist shoulders a huge burden: objectivity. How do we keep our own values out of the process of creating reliable knowledge? How do we maintain creativity while focusing on evidence? How do we avoid infringing on values when conducting scholarship?

Fortunately, the process of science encapsulates a series of steps that prevents or minimizes the intrusion of bias and personal values. This is one feature that distinguishes science from other "ways of knowing." I wrote about this process using simple language in a peer-reviewed journal many years ago. I taught relevant concepts for more than two decades, and I wrote about it as introductory material in several books. My presentation of this information largely missed the proverbial mark, which comes as no surprise in retrospect. After all, most people within this culture are unfamiliar with science and how it works. As such, many people routinely refer to science as a belief system on a par with religion. Some even incorrectly call it a cult.

For the most part, in other words, science is misunderstood. It is small wonder rational behavior is rare, even vanishing, in a culture of greed, material pursuits, and celebrity worship.

As humans, scientists are not immune from bias. Nor are scientists free from values (fortunately). When they are conducting science, scientists follow a process intended to negate their biases and their values. Hence are some scientists able to pursue paranormal beliefs at home while also conducting legitimate science in the laboratory. In other words, a scientist can be a follower of an Abrahamic religion without invoking gawd or a miracle to explain extraordinary observations.

In a similar manner, a scientist can be an activist. My own activism is inspired by my scientific activities, and my life as a rationalist is influenced by my activism.

As with any legitimate scientist, I am open to being incorrect. Openness to the public correction of errors is among the greatest characteristics of science. Try correcting a religious leader in public for a quick lesson on ego in the absence of evidence.

Non-attachment to a particular outcome is a primary tenet of science, as with the philosophy of Buddhism. In addition, separating a scientist, or anybody else, from his or her work goes a long way toward accumulating meaningful information. In other words, a scientist acting within the realm of science is under no burden at all.

I have endured seemingly endless bleating about gawd, aliens, The Powers That Be, and other entities who "would not let humans go extinct." This, of course, is irrational. It assumes somebody or something is controlling Earth's thermostat. It presumes knowledge without evidentiary support.

Science is not a religion. Science is not technology. Science is not what it produces. Science is a way of knowing far superior to other known processes of acquiring information with respect to the production of reliable knowledge. I suspect most readers will have no idea what these words mean.

It is obviously too late for rationalism to positively influence this culture. Is it too late to influence you? I suspect the answer depends upon at least two things: (1) the depth and breadth of your cultural programming, and (2) your willingness to learn.

## Seven Threes

Imagine you are listening to the radio as you gaze at the horizon from your fourth-floor window. You see a mushroom cloud and immediately recognize it as the detonation from a nuclear bomb. You realize the 20-foot I-beam spinning toward you will strike you dead in three seconds. There is no way to escape. You simply wait.

You miscalculated the path of the I-beam. It sails overhead, narrowly missing the roof above your head.

The voice on the radio announces the bomb blast will level everything in the city in three minutes. Compared to three seconds, three minutes seems like an eternity. What will you do with the time? Make a telephone call? Make peace with your god?

Now imagine a trip to the medical doctor. He matter-of-factly informs you that your condition gives you only three minutes to live. He leaves you alone with your thoughts. You ponder your life and wonder how to proceed. You think about calling somebody. Or maybe you will take a few deep breaths instead.

The doctor reenters the examination room after two minutes and thirty seconds. He apologizes for his error and says you have about three hours to live, not three minutes. You breathe a sigh of relief. Three hours seems a long time compared to three minutes. You can make a few calls, pen a quick will, and record a few thoughts on paper for posterity.

Rinse and repeat for a diagnosis of three days versus three hours. Then do the same for three weeks instead of three days. Three weeks! It is nearly an eternity compared to a few days.

Three weeks does not seem long until it is compared to a few days. Ditto for three months relative to three weeks. Also, three years compared to three months.

Three years is a short-term, terminal diagnosis. Few people would be satisfied to learn they have such a short future.

I doubt many people reading these words have three years to live. Habitat for humans on Earth will disappear shortly after the Arctic ice is gone, probably 2019 or 2020. Three decades is a pipe dream that will be experienced by no humans now on Earth.

Although three years is a stunningly short span of time, it does not seem at all short relative to three months. Ditto for the comparisons of months to weeks to days to hours to minutes to seconds. Thus, the seven threes, from seconds to years, serve as a powerful reminder to live in the present moment.

We do not have long. *Pressum Diem*! May we find the means and the fortitude to squeeze the life out of every moment.

## *Pursuing Excellence: An Exercise*

Because we do not have long to live, I suggest an exercise to help the reader in her pursuit of excellence. The exercise is modified from one sent me by my friend Bill Lott.

Start with about 50 blank index cards. Carry a few index cards and a pen or pencil at all times. Responses to the following will appear at any time, consistent with what Albert Einstein called, "The three Bs": His ideas often came when he was in the bathroom, bedroom, or bus.

Constantly have in mind the following four questions: (1) What can I hardly wait to do? (2) What has brought me great joy in the past? (3) What have I done in the past that brought joy to others? (4) What do I think is the meaning or purpose of my life?

When inspiration strikes, place the answer on a blank index card. When you have written on at least 50 cards, in a day or several months, spread them out on a tabletop, create clusters of similar answers and find patterns among the clusters.

The idea is to use as many such cards as possible to create the most accurately meaningful clusters and patterns. As a result, you are encouraged to continue the process and repeat the exercise every time you accumulate at least 50 completed cards in days, weeks, or months.

# Chapter 4: Authority, Evidence, and Conservation Biology

*We will gradually become indifferent to what goes on in the minds of other people when we acquire an adequate knowledge of the superficial and futile nature of their thoughts, of the narrowness of their views, of the paltriness of their sentiments, of the perversity of their opinions, and of the number of their errors... We shall then see that whoever attaches a lot of value to the opinions of others pays them too much honor.*

(Arthur W. Schopenhauer)

In the occasional fit of hubris, I claim to be the world's leading authority on near-term human extinction as a result of abrupt climate change. In return, I am subject to frequent personal attacks. This chapter provides a partial response, beginning with a screed and including a glimpse into my transparent life.

## A Screed

I will start with a few definitions. Each is selected as the most relevant example from the Merriam-Webster online dictionary.

*Authority*: an individual cited or appealed to as an expert

*Near:* not far away in time

*Term*: a limited or definite extent of time; especially ... the time for which something lasts

*Human*: of, relating to, or characteristic of humans

*Extinction*: the act of making extinct or causing to be extinguished.

*Abrupt*: lacking smoothness or continuity

*Climate*: the average course or condition of the weather at a place usually over a period of years as exhibited by temperature, wind velocity, and precipitation

*Change*: to make different in some particular

As a result of these definitions, I claim to be an authority on the topic of near-term human extinction as a result of abrupt climate change. It is hardly a wild claim, considering the frequency with which I am asked to speak and write about this topic. The topic itself is defined simply by combining a few words in simple, straightforward fashion.

I am routinely criticized for my predictions, despite the strong supporting evidence underlying them. Predictions are an important part of the scientific endeavor, as I indicated in the prior chapter. I stand by my predictions, which are likely conservative, based on contemporary evidence.

I am not now suggesting, nor have I ever suggested, that authority supersedes evidence. I rely upon evidence as the basis for my articles and public presentations. The evidence I present can be checked for its veracity in future chapters of this book, as well as in *Extinction Dialogs* (co-authored by Carolyn Baker) and numerous posts at my weblog, Nature Bats Last (guymcpherson.com).

My work quotes actual science, supported by actual evidence. The evidence has grown considerably during the last few years. I am not making up this stuff. I am not, to quote one of the more impolite, misinformed readers of my work, "...advocating highly unscientific specific dates for NTE" (near-term extinction). No evidence is presented, as usual, to support the insult, which included the charge of charlatanism. Considering I do not earn money from my work, calling me a charlatan seems nearly as absurd as making accusations without supporting evidence. Indeed, one could argue that I once was "a person who falsely pretends to know or be something in order to deceive people." But I left my high-pay, low-work position at a major university to pursue an honest country living in May of 2009.

Indeed, I routinely read that my work is rooted in money. This claim, while false, is not surprising. After all, most people work for one reason: money.

Lacking passion, lacking purpose, the vast majority of people within this culture chase money for one reason: necessity. This is what they have always done. This is what the culture "forces" them to do. This is what "everybody" does.

Were I motivated by money, I never would have pursued an academic life. Initially, such a life is an intellectually grueling existence for a modest wage. In addition, were I motivated by money, I certainly never would have left that life. I was comfortably ensconced in the privileged position of tenured full professor for which I was paid a comfortable salary and not required to teach. I could have easily put my life on cruise control and lived out my days traveling the world and otherwise pursuing the life of my dreams.

Money does not define me. Lack of money constrains my ability to conduct my work. It does not constrain my ability to conduct my life.

I no longer earn money from the books I have written and edited. Initially, I earned royalties of about fifty cents per (new) copy sold. These payments totaled a few hundred dollars per year during the best of times. That was before the publishers of all my recent books declared bankruptcy. I write because my message is important, not because it is lucrative.

I do not earn money with my public speaking. Rather, every tour costs me more than is returned via donations. I tour to speak because my message is important, not because touring is lucrative. On the contrary, it is physically and emotionally grueling.

Were it not for the frugal life I have conducted, along with the generosity of partners, friends, and supporters, I would have been living even closer to the monetary edge for the last several years. My point: My message matters. It matters to me considerably more than luxury. It also matters to others, if I am to believe the positive feedback I receive every day.

Does my message matter to you? My answer is, ironically, modified from a bumper sticker: Acceptance of abrupt climate change is optional, although participation is mandatory.

*Cui bono?* Who benefits from my message? Only the willing.

In contrast to the baseless charges to which I have become accustomed, I provide evidence in my attempts to educate the clueless masses. I realize this approach is contrary to the dominant thinking (sic) in this culture. I also realize the difficulty in this culture of distinguishing charlatans from purveyors of evidence. A culture based on lies and patriarchy is appreciated, at least by lying patriarchs, even though the lies and patriarchy are rarely acknowledged.

As always, I welcome any corrections of my errors, although they are rarely offered. I would love to be wrong about near-term human extinction, not to mention habitat loss for the many non-human species this culture gleefully drives to extinction. I would love to believe the Sixth Mass Extinction is a myth. Unfortunately, I know better.

People filled with fear rarely agree with me. Ditto for people filled with hope, wishes, or dreams. Ditto for engineers, infamous for their techno-fixes that notoriously exacerbate every problem and predicament of significance.

Comprehension is rare, understanding rarer still. Knowledge often brings isolation in a culture characterized by denial. It also brings liberation. Most prefer the self-induced shackles that enable them to ignore or modify the evidence.

Few things are more painful than describing the reality unseen by the willfully ignorant masses. Few appreciate a truth-teller in his own time. Evidence is deemed irrelevant in a culture constructed from lies. *Ad hominem* comments prevail, and those who launch insults suffer no consequences. Such is the online, "civilized" life. As Arthur Schopenhauer pointed out, "To truth only a brief celebration of victory is allowed between the two long periods during which it is condemned as paradoxical, or disparaged as trivial."

# Picking Cherries

I am routinely accused of cherry picking information about climate change. I plead guilty, with the following 1,000-word disclaimer and recognition that everybody else picks cherries, too. One of the differences between me and the others: I admit my bias, and they claim to have none.

I will start with a line from recently deceased professor emeritus and long-time teacher Albert Bartlett: "The greatest shortcoming of the human race is our inability to understand the exponential function." When I speak and write about climate change, most members of the audience are stuck in fifth grade, unaware that nature often exhibits non-linearity.

Imagine you shop at your local grocery store. You buy bread from the bread aisle, which actually only takes up half an aisle. Little do you realize that the grocery store is transitioning into a bread store, so the manager will double the amount of bread in the store each day. By the time you return to the store, a week after you found the bread in the expected location, more than half the aisles now have bread. Only bread. Had you come a day later, the transition would have been complete. The days of buying rice, beans, and laundry detergent are gone. Welcome to the exponential function, an example of non-linearity.

I pick cherries because I see nobody else connecting the dots on climate change. I see nobody else making an honest effort to describe our predicament. So, by default, I collate, summarize, and synthesize information about climate change.

This planet has become so Orwellian that those who collate the facts and pass them along are hated as liars.

I see plenty of support for denying the obvious. Almost everybody reading these words has a vested interest in not wanting to think about climate change, which helps explain why the climate-change deniers have won the information wars. According to a December, 2013 paper in *Climatic Change*, the climate change counter-movement is funded to the tune of nearly a billion dollars each year. In the United States, Americans continue to brag about their prowess in destroying the living planet long after a few of us recognized the irony of claiming success by grinding the living planet into dust. The story is similar in other industrialized countries.

How obvious is ongoing climate change induced by anthropogenic global warming? If you are unwilling to look outside, consider that abnormal is the new normal, and we are just getting started. A paper by Katharine Ricke and Ken Caldeira published in the 3 December 2014 issue of *Environmental Research Letters* indicates that maximum warming from carbon dioxide emissions occurs about a decade after the emissions occur. Rising emissions during each of the last many decades points to a truly catastrophic future, and not long from now. There is nothing to be done today to undo what we did during the last decade. In addition, abrupt, dramatic changes in climate clearly are part of the ongoing and near-term scenario.

This knowledge brings with it horror and relief. I am, of course, horrified by what is to come, which includes the near-certainty of the near-term collapse of civilization and subsequent human extinction. Largely unafflicted by the arrogance of humanism, I can only imagine the attendant short-term alleviation of oppression on the few remaining non-human species before their habitat disappears, too. Industrial civilization is destroying every aspect of the living planet, and I know virtually nobody who wants to stop the runaway train. Yes, collapse of civilization will destroy habitat for humans and ultimately it will kill us. Our deaths are guaranteed regardless, unless I missed a memo.

I have given up on "civilized" humans making any effort to take relevant action. Never mind our stunning myopia: The money to be made is clearly more important than the extinctions we cause, including our own.

As pointed out in the March, 2012 issue of *Nature Climate Change*, several psychological reasons explain why people have a hard time dealing with the stark reality of climate change. David Roberts comments at length in his resulting article in *Grist*, published 27 July 2012:

1. To the extent that climate change is an abstract concept, it is non-intuitive and cognitively difficult to grasp.
2. Our moral judgment system is finely tuned to react to intentional transgressions – not unintentional ones.

3. Things that make us feel guilty provoke self-defensive mechanisms.
4. Uncertainty breeds wishful thinking, so the lack of definitive prognoses results in unreasonable optimism.
5. Our division into moral and political tribes generates ideological polarization; climate change becomes politicized.
6. Events do not seem urgent when they seem to be far away in time and space; out-group victims fall by the wayside.

At considerable risk of pummeling the dead equine, I will reiterate a couple of paragraphs I pointed out in one of my earlier books, *Extinction Dialogs*: Leading mainstream, corporate outlets routinely to lie to the public. According to a report published 11 January 2014, "The BBC has spent tens of thousands of pounds over six years trying to keep secret an extraordinary 'eco' conference which has shaped its coverage of global warming." At the 2006 event, green activists and scientists -- one of whom believes climate change is a bigger danger than global nuclear war -- lectured 28 of the BBC's most senior executives.

Indeed, mainstream scientists minimize the message at every turn. As we have known for years, scientists almost invariably underplay climate impacts. I am not implying conspiracy among scientists. Science selects for conservatism. Academia selects for extreme conservatism. These folks are loath to risk drawing undue attention to themselves by pointing out there might be a threat to civilization. Never mind the near-term threat to our entire species (almost none could care less about other species). If the truth is dire, they can find another, not-so-dire version. This concept is supported in an article by Keynyn Brysse and colleagues in the February, 2013 issue of *Global Environmental Change* pointing out that climate-change scientists routinely underestimate impacts "...by erring on the side of least drama."

In other words, science selects for conservatism (aka picking cherries long after they ripen). Science, after all, is merely the process of elucidating the obvious. Climate-change scientists routinely underestimate impacts "by erring on the side of least drama" (aka looking for the cherries long after they have fallen off the tree, onto the ground, and been consumed by rodents).

The feedbacks are too numerous, the inertia too strong. The corporate media and corporate governments of the world keep lying, and too few have held them accountable.

# *Distinguishing a Person from His or Her Work*

Separating a person from his or her work is difficult. We are inclined to throw out the proverbial baby with the dirty water. When we learn a celebrity is flawed, we tend to dismiss her work, at least temporarily. The other approach, probably more common in this culture, is to deny the celebrity's flaws.

Ignorance is bliss. Bliss is the state preferred by the masses.

Consider a few examples. Edward Abbey was widely regaled as a thinker, public speaker, and writer. He was among the early philosopher-poets to strongly link social justice and environmental protection. According to rumors, he was a slumlord with a sordid history of relations with young women. He married several times, each time to a woman in her twenties or younger. His actions, at least on some occasions, were beyond societal norms -- oh, the horrors -- and also beyond what many people would consider ethical.

Abbey's writing is thoughtful, provocative, and timely nearly three decades after his death. He and Doug Peacock are the only writers who make me want to put down their books ... and take a hike.

I love Abbey's work. I doubt I would have loved the man, whose work hinted broadly at misogyny and patriarchy. Unfortunately -- or perhaps not -- we never met. I cannot know how I would have felt about Abbey the person.

In the wake of his 2016 death, I read many horrible tales about singer/songwriter David Bowie (née David Robert Jones). Some of the stories are almost certainly accurate. Yet he was still a superb practitioner of his chosen craft.

Many people continue to vote, knowing they are voting for a successful, serial liar. When people vote, they balance the lies told -- and the ones yet to come -- with the presumed effectiveness of the candidate of choice. I doubt anybody is naive enough to expect the full truth from any politician.

Ours is one of the few species known to lie overtly via voice, and we make up for all the nonhuman species that cannot utter an untruth. James Halperin's 1999 science fiction novel, *Truth Machine*, tackles the issue of the lies we all tell by creating a society in which every lie is detected immediately. As you can imagine, society is turned upside-down in a very brief period.

No more asking if this dress makes me look fat. No more false flattery. No more "little white lies" to make people feel better. No more denying the total costs of grid-tied electricity, food at the grocery stores, and water pouring from the municipal taps. Only the cold, naked truths remain.

For better and worse, and perhaps only via willful ignorance, we usually distinguish a man from his work (and a woman, too). If we knew the details of the personal lives of our heroes, I doubt we would sincerely admire anybody for long.

An obvious exception is the customary treatment of whistleblowers. If few appreciate the message, then even fewer want to believe it. The majority denies the message and castigates the messenger. If the message is too dire -- in other words if it threatens to interfere with monetary gain for the financially wealthy -- the messenger is silenced.

Of course, silencing the messenger does not change the message. Doing so, however, slows the rate of transmission while allowing positive emotions to the ignorant masses. Such an outcome provides a temporary victory for the majority, with truth as the only cost. The dominant culture and the masses who serve it are only rarely concerned with evidence. Ergo, silencing the messenger *IS* victory, albeit in pyrrhic form.

And who among us does not appreciate a warm campfire on a cold night? Tall tales, true or not, add to the feel-good memories. Internalized warmth thus nicely accompanies the campfire's heat.

As with most issues, radicalization is a difficult path, discouraged and disparaged by contemporary society. Digging beneath the surface has its rewards. Comfort is rarely one of them.

On a few uncommon occasions, a person becomes indistinguishable from his or her work. Consider, as one example, nutritionist Dr. Gary Null. He is in the uncomfortable position of being unable to die. He must live forever. The day he dies, no matter his age or general health in the preceding moments, is the day most people will conclude nutrition is irrelevant to health. In other words, Null's death proves him wrong.

In contrast to Dr. Null, my own death, immediately attributable to abrupt climate change, proves me right. Sadly, I will be unable to say, "I told you so."

I am not proud of some of my personal actions. Yet I believe my scientific work has great integrity. The discriminating reader will differentiate with ease Guy

McPherson the person from Guy McPherson's analyses, public speaking, and written works.

Guy McPherson just referred to himself in the third person. It was weird.

# Who Am I, Anyway?

Authority is one of the pillars of patriarchy. I recall one of my colleagues telling me, more than 15 years ago on the campus in Utah where he taught biology, about the majority of his college students citing God and their father as two of the three authorities he requested for an introductory writing project.

Need more be said?

In a culture of celebrity, as epitomized in the United States and exemplified by the "first" world, evidence is perceived by the masses as secondary to authority. If Lady Gaga says something, regardless of how obviously ridiculous the statement, then it must be "true." As a renowned public figure, Lady Gaga is somehow viewed as a credible source, regardless of the topic. She can sing. She can talk. Therefore, she must know more about politics and science than the majority.

Sadly, I suspect she does. She is literate, after all.

I am attacked, insulted, libeled, and slandered every day because I present evidence people do not want to accept. the *evidence* is not questioned because it is unimpeachable. There is no credible critique of my work. Every aspect of my personal life, no matter how irrelevant, is dragged into the conversation. It is the opposite of the Lady Gaga phenomenon.

A radical since my teens, I get to the root of issues that matter through my teaching, research, and social criticism. One result: I have repeatedly been asked to serve as an expert witness in the United States judicial system.

I walk my talk. When evidence indicated the collapse of civilization would allow our species and others a longer run on Earth, I voluntarily walked away from my high-pay, low-work position as a revered professor at a major university. I created an off-grid homestead and transformed myself from an ignorant city dweller to a multi-talented grower, builder, and communicator. Too late, journal articles about global dimming told me I had made a tremendous mistake. The principled move from Tucson, Arizona to the wilds of southern New Mexico cost me everything except my integrity. Whether it was "worth it" no longer matters. It is done.

As a long-time radical, I know about evidence. I have taught courses in the philosophy of science and the generation of reliable knowledge. I was acknowledged in my home college as an A+ Advisor my third year on campus, and I suspect I am the only person ever honored with the highest award given by each of the two transdisciplinary colleges at the University of Arizona (Graduate College 2002, Honors College 2009). I am one of the few people in history to achieve the status of full professor before turning 40 years of age. My lengthy resume is replete with scholarly publications, including dozens of peer-reviewed journal articles (the "gold standard" by which the process of science creates reliable knowledge).

Seeing a single paper through the publication process requires talent and persistence. Essentially, none of my critics have accomplished this task. Collating and synthesizing evidence in the form of a book is beyond even most academics, especially in the natural sciences. My scholarly efforts have produced more than a dozen books.

I know about conservation biology and climate change, too. I have been studying both topics since my early days in graduate school in the early 1980s. My list of publications includes peer-reviewed journal articles in premiere ecological journals describing interactions between climate change and ecosystems.

As a result of my knowledge of conservation biology and climate change, I have become the world's leading authority on the topic of abrupt climate change leading to near-term human extinction. Consequently, I have been featured in several documentary films, as well as an episode of *National Geographic Explorer* with Bill Nye, the other science guy. I am a frequent interviewee for broadcast and print media.

Few people accuse their oncologist of profiting after she issues a fatal diagnosis. Once the patient recovers from the shock, he sometimes thanks the honest doctor. If said medical doctor misunderstands the evidence and offers an incorrect, hopeful diagnosis, then filing a legal claim of malpractice is warranted. Indeed, it is expected in the United States, the most litigious society in the history of the planet.

I pursue and promote the truth, based upon evidence. The evidence comes primarily, and almost exclusively, from the very conservative peer-reviewed journal *Literature*. I am *NOT* referring to *MY* truth, a notion rooted in the naively postmodern palaver that we each have our own truth and that each version of the truth is equally valid. Nor am I referring to the evidence-free religious concept of Truth rooted in patriarchy.

My detractors include unscientific people afraid to face evidence, lovers of the life-destroying heat engine known as civilization, and others who lack the credentials necessary to collate and organize relevant evidence. Few people turn to their electrician for advice about cancer. Yet many people seek and believe diagnoses about climate change from wholly unqualified sources.

I am routinely accused of horrible intentions and terrible acts. There is no supporting evidence. None is needed when the hate is spewed online from a culture dominated by willfully ignorant, small-minded people with questionable intelligence writing for an audience with similar talents. I dare not fully venture into the topic of trolls paid to deny reality and promote disaster capitalism no matter the cost.

My work relies on evidence. It is rooted in reason. I am a rationalist. Contrary to the cries from my critics, ever eager to attack the messenger rather than evaluate the message, I am not mentally ill. The entire culture is insane. The inmates operating the asylum, believe they are the sane ones.

I have been deemed insane since voluntarily leaving my high-pay, low-work position at a major research university. Taking action based on principle, rather than money, seems crazy to people afflicted with a bad case of the dominant paradigm.

In contrast to my critics, I do not benefit from my work in any way. It has cost me thousands of dollars for every dollar I have received in return. It has cost me the ability to do what I love. It has cost me everybody I loved from my former life.

I am strongly motivated by evidence. In presenting the results, in simple language, I make the evidence accessible to the public.

I am not ignorant enough to believe my detractors will pull in their talons. I am not sufficiently deluded to believe the attacks will cease until human extinction is complete. I am under no impression that reason will prevail before the last human on Earth takes her last breath. The grip of patriarchy is strong. There is no escape at a scale that matters. The only way out is in.

# The Road to Academic Success

Most people receive information primarily from corporate sources. For the relatively few people who actually read, the usual publications include newspapers and magazines such as *Newsweek, Time,* and *People.* These publications are churned out by corporations to entertain the masses and sell products. They have proven remarkably successful on both fronts.

There are many differences between these conventional magazines and peer-reviewed publications. Most notably, authors of the latter publications pay to have their work printed in outlets that are expensive to purchase. Furthermore, results are published *once* in the journal literature, whereas every catchy "news" item is spewed ad nauseum by the corporate media. In addition, the processes by which the two disparate publications see the light of day are quite different. I elaborate below.

Consider, by way of example, the prestigious journal *Proceedings of the National Academy of Sciences* (PNAS), the official scientific journal of the National Academy of Sciences (NAS). The NAS is not in the business of making money, and publishing is an expensive undertaking. As a result, as with most peer-reviewed journals, authors pay a fee to have a paper published. The fee, called "page charges," typically is based upon the length of the final publication. In other words, authors of journal articles do not get paid to publish their work. Rather, they -- or, more often their institution or the grants they have worked diligently to secure -- bear the monetary cost of publishing their results.

Imagine a freelance journalist having to pay *Time* for the honor of appearing in print. Under this imaginary scenario, the world would soon be devoid of freelance journalists.

Another significant difference between the two kinds of publications is the process by which a paper appears in print. In the case of *Newsweek, Time,* and *People,* a staff writer or freelance journalist pitches an idea to an editor. Once the idea is approved, research is conducted and the story is written (it is not as if the process is as easy and fun as this cryptic description makes it seem). If the result meets journalistic standards for ethics and credibility, and also has the all-important ability to attract readers and, therefore, advertising dollars, the paper is approved for print by an editor. The editor need not, and probably does not, know much about the topic. Contrast this approach with the customary approach taken in the arena of peer-reviewed journals.

In the case of **PNAS**, and most other peer-reviewed journals, the idea for the final published work is vetted in the scientific community in many deliberate and time-consuming ways. The initial germ of an idea is discussed with colleagues on campus and during conferences. It is scrutinized and put to a test, the nature of which often requires years of research in the laboratory and in the field (aka the actual world). Results are evaluated with detailed measurements. Numbers are crunched using a stunningly sophisticated array of computational methods and devices. Initial results are presented to colleagues via seminars on campus and then at conferences. Every conceivable error is sought by critical audiences eager to find fault with new information. Finally, the written results are submitted to a journal for consideration. The fun ends here.

The submitted draft is read by an editor with expertise in the field. In general, and to keep this description simple, s/he has a couple of options: (1) reject the paper as inappropriate for the journal or lacking in substance, or (2) accept the draft on behalf of PNAS, and send it to subject-matter specialists. Either way, a confirmatory note is sent to the author who has taken on the task as the corresponding author for the paper. Obviously, rejecting the paper means the end of this story for this paper in this journal. The authors can call an end to this project, after years of scholarly work, or they can submit the paper, generally after many hours of additional scholarship, to a different journal. If the latter route is chosen, the scholarly version of "rinse and repeat" begins.

If the paper is accepted for review, then it is sent to reviewers. These are the experts on this particular topic who directly compete with authors of the submitted paper for funding and prestige. Three or four of them typically are selected by the editor. Their names are not revealed to the authors of the paper under consideration as part of a process called "blind review." Increasingly in the social sciences, and very rarely in the natural sciences, double-blind review is used (in which the author's names are redacted by the editor before the paper is sent to reviewers). Bear in mind that all reviewers are selected because they are renowned in their field of study. They are busy. They are not paid to review the work of their colleagues. One could argue they are rewarded for providing a late, scathing review or no review at all. I have seen years-old manuscripts on the desks of former colleagues, promised for review in two weeks.

Once the editor receives detailed reviews, often after harassing unpaid, busy reviewers for several months or years, s/he is charged with making a decision that falls into one of four categories (I am lumping, not splitting): (1) reject the submission as unsuitable for this journal, with no opportunity for additional consideration, (2) reject the paper as submitted, with an opportunity for submitting it again once various criteria are met, (3) accept the paper, conditional upon responding to criticisms raised by reviewers (which could include abundant additional research), or (4) accept the paper as written (the equivalent of opening a book in a large library and having several thousand dollars fall out). In my lengthy academic career, I had each of these experiences (the latter only once, with a journal lacking stature, and I would have preferred the thousands of dollars). The middle two outcomes are most common, in large part because academics soon learn how to avoid option (1) and few are lucky and skilled enough to experience option (4). The process from the germination of a new idea to the resulting peer-reviewed publication, depending upon the required infrastructure and observations, typically requires between a year and a decade. Stunningly to me, my academic work continues to be cited frequently.

There is a striking difference between conventional, corporate publications with which most people are familiar and peer-reviewed publications. The former are designed to make money for the corporations publishing them. The latter are designed to generate reliable knowledge for the informed citizenry and are appreciated only by curious trackers of truth. Edward Bernays loved the former, as indicated by his thoughts about the news: "But being dependent, every day of the year and for year after year, upon certain politicians for news, the newspaper reporters are obliged to work in harmony with their news sources."

## The Relevance of Conservation Biology

The multidisciplinary enterprise of conservation biology is helpful in understanding the concept of near-term human extinction. The pillars of conservation biology -- speciation, extinction, and habitat -- are poorly understood by most scientists, yet they are crucial to understanding and predicting the demise of organisms, including *Homo sapiens.*

Conservation biologists are reluctant to apply words such as "field" or "discipline" to their collective endeavor because these words are deemed too narrow to be accurate. Conservation biology draws from several subjects to tackle complex topics such as guild, niche, functional extinction, and species diversity. I would be hard-pressed to think of an endeavor that requires a broader understanding than conservation biology. A mix of theory and its application makes conservation biology simultaneously difficult to categorize -- much less to understand by those unfamiliar with the relevant vocabulary -- and crucial to the preservation of life on Earth.

Conservation biologists readily understand the fragile nature of life. We know the importance of soil, wind, fire, precipitation, temperature, bacteria, fungi, and myriad other factors on the continued persistence of every life form. We study the importance of interspecific competition, mutualism, and evolution by natural selection. We are aware that every species continually dances on the edge of extinction, constantly hovering on the brink.

Extinction occurs when the last individual of a species dies. Most species are driven to extinction as a result of habitat loss. I suspect the final human will follow this path, not long after habitat is destroyed by abrupt climate change. A few species are hunted to extinction by humans. Violent though we can be, I doubt we join them.

Counting the losses is the saddest of jobs. As pointed out by Aldo Leopold, "One of the penalties of an ecological education is that one lives alone in a world of wounds." Few within civilization are aware of the horrors of civilization. They do not feel the wounds, for they are ignorant.

Conservation biology is the science of connecting seemingly disparate information to a clear, compelling story. It is the scientific study of the intricate, interconnected web comprising life on Earth. Disappearing birds, linked to disappearing insects, is one of the stories of conservation biology. That humans could be next is an obvious conclusion to every conservation biologist and stunningly few other people.

In sharp contrast to conservation biologists, engineers and CEOs are addicted to "fixing" rather than understanding. Furthermore, the culture in which we are embedded claims that quitters never win. Hollywood piles on with fantasies we love to believe. Even strategic retreat is disparaged by the patriarchs this society heralds as "winners." The most deluded of these people incorrectly believe we can build our way out of extinction. More and bigger buildings surely will pave the way -- irony intended -- to a brighter future characterized by bigger, better, faster, and more. What could possibly go wrong?

There are other reasons self-proclaimed scientists fail to address the most important topic in the history of our species. Privilege, including the attendant prestige and money, comes immediately to mind.

Considering the fantasy known as the dominant, infinite-growth paradigm, is it any wonder we cannot let go? Is it any wonder we deny death, at every level?

# How I Came to be So Hated

People often ask why I speak and write about abrupt climate change leading to near-term human extinction? If we cannot fix it, why bother knowing? Is it unclear who *WE* are or what it means to *FIX* this particular predicament?

Actually, people more frequently send me hate mail accusing me of profiting by lying about our demise than asking questions with civility. It is analogous to claiming a fire lookout gets paid by the number of fires she spots.

I wish. I wish I were lying. I wish I were profiting. Sadly, I am not. As science fiction writer Robert Heinlein pointed out, "Being right too soon is socially unacceptable."

I have no idea why I am compelled to defend my conclusions, all of which are supported by abundant evidence. I suppose my inner teacher believes I can overcome profound, willful ignorance with evidence. This thought alone indicates my unrepentant optimism regarding the human condition.

My detractors include unscientific people afraid to face evidence, lovers of the destructive heat engine known as civilization, and others who lack the credentials necessary to collate and organize relevant evidence. Few people turn to their plumber for advice about cancer, yet they are perfectly willing to accept information from unqualified people about climate change and its impacts on habitat for organisms.

Were I better-known, I suspect I would make the list of finalists among the most-hated people in the world. It is a goal, in any event.

That is a joke, of course. If I do not point it out, every time, it will be turned against me.

As I have been pointing out for years, people are stupid. Most people, most of the time. Present readership excluded, of course.

Among the offenders are offensively ignorant and ill-informed, office-bound modelers who inexplicably believe field observations ought to fit models, rather than the reverse. Among the worst offenders are armchair prognosticators with video cameras and the ability to post online their ever-changing opinions unattached to evidence. Field observations and peer-reviewed journal literature are anathema to those who promote the dominant narrative. The latter notably include the folks who benefit from the life-crushing heat engine to which we affectionately refer as "civilization."

The "best" critiques of my work are an ancient series of *ad hominem* attacks disguised as blog posts. They tend to be written by self-proclaimed science educators without Ph.D. degrees. Rarely is thought given to lack of credentials, motives, the unprofessional quality of analyses, or the dated nature of the work. Other critics post on blogs or selfie videos, presumably to counter the hundreds of journal articles on which I rely.

I have been called a narcissist, among many other terrible names. Technically, the term is "narcissistic personality disorder," a mental disorder in which people have an inflated sense of their own importance, a deep need for admiration, and a lack of empathy for others. My customary detractors cannot be bothered with proper use of the English language.

It began as libel. I turned it into a joke, as I often do. As a result, it became fodder for my detractors, based on ignorance and stupidity. Thus did my joke get turned on me. So much for playing Court Jester, one of my favorite tricks.

First, I will provide a little background about the narcissist story, then a bit of personal history, followed finally by the evidence. I suspect the typical reader will be least interested in the latter. Evidence is ignored or worse in a culture infatuated with celebrities. As suggested by Isaac Asimov -- and many others, before and after him -- the typical American reader is woefully, ignorant and sufficiently stupid to believe his or her own opinion is superior to any evidence s/he encounters. A fitting line from Asimov accurately describes the worsening situation in America: "There is a cult of ignorance in the United States, and there has always been. The strain of anti-intellectualism has been a constant thread winding its way through our political and cultural life, nurtured by the false notion that democracy means that 'my ignorance is just as good as your knowledge.'"

My detractors grab onto anything that might prove me wrong. They do not know enough about the process of science to understand terms such as *Proof, Fact, Theory,* and *Evidence* as applied within the realm of science. Do not even get me started on the postmodern palaver of everybody has his/her own truth, an idea rooted in exceptionalism that promotes abandoning personal responsibility. I will not take the time within this short volume for a course in *Introduction to Scientific Terminology,* a course badly needed and seldom offered on contemporary college campuses. I taught such material for years, in yet another case of a slim minority failing to keep up with a rising tide.

I have been the target of this type of nonsense for years. Surprisingly, I am not yet accustomed to it. For example, I was diagnosed by my so-called colleagues with a rare brain disease when I left active service at the university in 2009. Apparently, only insanity would drive a full professor to leave a high-pay, no-work position in exchange for an escape from the heat engine known as civilization. The attempt to escape an asylum run by its inmates seemed a rational approach at the time, even though it failed in my case.

I was diagnosed as a narcissist in 2016 by people, including former friends, who could not distinguish me from my work. Feebly latching onto a label, the offenders in question indicated the evidence I collated was rooted in narcissism. Perhaps you see the problem. Perhaps not. Going a step further, the detractors claimed my ill-advised attempt to attract attention was motivating my collation, organization, and synthesis of the evidence. To some people, this actually makes sense. Asimov's quote applies particularly well to these people.

Turning the libelous comment into a joke, as I am inclined to do with insults launched my way, was a mistake on my part. It was a humorous attempt to make fun of the libel and also to make fun of those people for whom such libelous comments make sense. It is consistent with my pattern of overestimating the intelligence of my audience, contrary to a line attributed to, and probably paraphrased from, H.L. Mencken: "Nobody ever went broke underestimating the intelligence of the American public." My pattern of overestimating the intelligence of my audience doubtless contributed to my going broke.

My Camus-inspired, absurdist outlook on the universe routinely has me turning everything into a joke. I suspect the typical person in this culture has no idea what the prior sentence means.

The joke went south. Soon after, people were claiming that I admit my narcissism. Well, I do: *as a joke!* As should be clear with the application of a small amount of logic, no narcissist would admit to being a narcissist, much less make the proclamation before an audience. Logic is an attribute possessed by few within contemporary culture.

I have no doubt my detractors will continue to use my humor against me. Indeed, early during 2017, a woman claiming to love me -- and the people on that list is quite different from the same list a few years ago, when the collegiate accolades were still coming my way -- sent me an email message in which she pointed out her love for me and then, a few lines later, referred to the "well known (sic) admittance of your narcissism" (sic). She went on to explain to me that I had not done the requisite work in building my human community, thereby ignoring the thousands of hours I contributed exactly to this cause during my life, and quite recently with my former tribe in New Mexico. She has benefited directly from this work, and she continues to do so. This is yet another case of making my oft-repeated error of trusting "friends" with my thoughts. Far worse, I trusted them with my heart.

I continue to overestimate the intelligence of the populace, not to mention their empathy. I have a long history of incorporating the learning of empathy into my classrooms and presentations. My TEDx talk on the campus of Arizona State University in 2012 focused on this topic, which is consistent with my lifelong commitment to service. Such pursuits are clearly inconsistent with narcissistic personality disorder, which is characterized by "a lack of empathy for others." Considering my long-exhibited propensity toward empathy for others -- including non-human species -- the charge of narcissism seems especially incoherent and mean-spirited. Yet I am not surprised.

A quick look at the other two elements of narcissistic personality disorder, according to the Mayo Clinic, are "an inflated sense of their own importance" and "a deep need for admiration." The former is readily discounted with a close look at any one of my dozens of public presentations in which I point out the insignificance of the human experience, and also by my oft-stated weak will to live. Had I a "deep need for admiration," I would never focus my presentations on the most-dreaded topic in the world.

My attempts to respond kindly sometimes fail, although I can and do distinguish between being nice and being kind. In contrast to the mass of humans I encounter, I recognize niceness and kindness are sometimes mutually exclusive.

My inner teacher constantly struggles to get out.

No further elucidation is warranted regarding my extensive body of work. None will suffice for those who deny evidence. I will continue my attempts to disengage from discussions operating strictly within an evidence-free zone, recognizing that such a step will nullify nearly every prospective conversation.

Hatred will continue to flow my way, not because of evidence, but rather because of the opposite: It is more comfortable to deny evidence than to ponder one's own death. The processes of cultural "dumbing down" and appreciation -- even glorification -- of ignorance and stupidity have led to our demise. How could it have been otherwise?

## More About Me and My Work

When I was a bright, inquisitive young boy, I was routinely told to work hard, to play by the rules, and to avoid arguing with adults. I was told to respect my elders. I was told arguing was impolite. I was also told to avoid people who acted differently from "normal" people.

Fast forward five decades to the nirvana of now. Nearly every day, I am criticized for failing to focus only on evidence. Nearly every day, I am asked to ignore emotions: "As a scientist, you need to stick to science."

Rarely does a day pass without criticism for failing to serve as a personal therapist for people who have difficulty accepting the brevity of human life. Rarely does a day go by when I am not asked to address the emotional response to my message: "You cannot merely present the evidence and leave me on my own. You must tell me how to cope with my terminal diagnosis."

I am a scientist. I am not a therapist. I am a conservation biologist. I am not a counselor, shrink, or "life coach." And I am a human being, perennially grappling with the brevity of my own life, not to mention that of our species.

Few know more than I do about relationships gone awry, shattered by various toxic combinations of evidence and emotions. Few have given away so much of themselves or had more taken from them. What does my persistence reveal to you?

I have not received a paycheck for several years. I offer my work as a gift, freely available to all. Those who disagree with me are welcome to ignore my evidence-rich work.

I am more than willing to admit my insanity, at least compared to this profoundly sick society. After all, genius and madness likely are inextricably, genetically linked. A line from gonzo American journalist Hunter S. Thompson comes to mind: "I wouldn't recommend sex, drugs or insanity for everyone, but they've always worked for me." Even more relevant, and less-known, are a few words from Aristotle: "There's a fine line between genius and insanity. I have erased this line."

Find a person who has given more in defense of Earth: privilege, position, fiat currency, relationships. Become that person. Perhaps then we can talk. Until then, you have work to do.

Again, I ask: What does my persistence in promulgating a message rooted in evidence reveal to you? Character? Will? Emotional instability? Genius? Insanity? Misguided radicalism? And what part of this whole affair is your business? Do you really want to spend your final days arguing with a man you have declared insane? Is that your own version of pursuing excellence?

So much drama in my life. So much discord. So much denial. So much hatred. So little time.

Decades after my bright and inquisitive nature was acknowledged, I still fit into both categories, if I do say so myself. Yet I am still searching for the "normal" people in this inane culture even as I continue to work hard and break all the societal rules I can.

Perhaps the optimists are correct, and this is the best of all possible worlds. Or maybe -- as J. Robert Oppenheimer pointed out -- the fears of the pessimists have come to pass and it is, indeed, the best of all possible worlds. Through either lens, this Earth is the one we have. Acceptance is a gift you give yourself. Only a fool would look a gift Earth in the mouth.

Privilege comes at a cost. The bill is long overdue.

"Civilization, like an airplane in flight, survives only as it keeps going forward." So wrote Edward Abbey, decades ago. My interpretation of Cactus Ed's line is akin to Jeff Goldblum's line in *Jurassic Park*: "Must go faster." This is a defining element of every civilization, including the current, industrialized version. Civilizations do not grow *or* die. They grow *and* die.

Growth is deemed necessary for this set of living arrangements. It is probably even true. More is better for cancer, civilizations, and the cancerous growth of industrial (sic) civilization (sic). The only quality worthy of mention is quantity. Everything, every *thing*, must be monetized. Grinding the living planet into dust is collateral damage for growth. The good of growth, like that of greed, is rarely questioned.

Every civilization reaches its end. In every case, the end is a surprise for most of the inhabitants. In most documented cases, a few individuals sounded the alarm as the proverbial ship was sinking. Those people were punished or ignored.

Every civilization is a wrecking ball in a crystal factory. The current version is the worst so far. With respect to pointing out those who benefit from civilization, I am a proud wrecking ball in a crystal factory.

Every species reaches its end. In every case, the last member of a species is unaware that he or she is the final version. We are the only species known to be aware of our demise at the level of a species. The few individuals sounding the alarm have been ignored, insulted, or punished.

Imagine any one of those people. Imagine their life's work.

Imagine every moment preparing for the current moment.

Imagine the enormity of sacrifice in pursuit of excellence. In pursuit of truth. In pursuit of love.

Imagine the life's work shattered. Imagine it gone awry.

Imagine it wounded, and then dead.

Imagine the life's work miscarried. No, worse: intentionally aborted by a homicidal maniac. Expecting more from a willfully ignorant populace blinded by greed is wishful thinking of the lowest order.

Now you are coming close to my world. It is a world dominated by reason and attacked without cause. For example, I tend to seek evidence from field researchers rather than from office-bound modelers and graduate students who rarely venture far from the city sidewalk. The latter people are quick to offer opinions unsupported by evidence. In contrast, my life as a field ecologist predisposes me toward an understanding of the natural world and away from fantasy technology. My professional life as a conservation biologist had me studying and teaching the three pillars upon which conservation biology is founded: speciation, extinction, and habitat.

It is not as if I am a failure in the academic world, as mentioned previously when describing my credentials and also my long list of publications. As I wrote, seeing a single paper through the publication process requires talent and persistence. Essentially, none of my critics has accomplished this task. Collating and synthesizing evidence in the form of a book is beyond even most academics, especially in the natural sciences. My scholarly efforts have produced more than a dozen books.

But, alas. The older I am, the better I was. I would guess that is the usual condition for people as they are looking back, grasping for meaning or long-lost glory. I am not interested in meaning derived from external sources. Life has only the meanings we assign it, and I am comfortable with the meanings of my life. As a result, I am comfortable in my own skin, a rare experience in this culture. Furthermore, past glory is just that: past.

Now I live for today, rather than in the past of my faulty memories or for the tomorrow that never comes. Call me a slow learner in a culture of *must go faster*. The speed of life, which often approaches the speed of light, is sufficiently exhilarating for me. Finally, I recognize that going faster is hazardous to non-human life and that it offers few rewards that matter (at least to me).

# The Long Odds Against My Being Here

I never imagined, at any possible level, I would wind up here. From the cosmos to my daily, mundane existence, my life is a testament to the absurdity of improbability.

As I have written and spoken many times, the existence of each of us is highly unlikely in the extreme. Our knowledge of the universe and DNA illustrates the long odds against any one of us appearing on this cosmic stage. Yet, in the face of these seemingly impossible odds, here we are. Not merely here, mind you. We are also here with brains big enough to contemplate how and why, along with powers of observation sufficient to invoke the notion of the miraculous.

As I was completing a mundane task, a friend who was helping brought up an anecdote from October, 1982 as a reminder of a stunningly improbable personal event. He said, "I'll bet you never thought you'd be doing *this* when you took that flier off the bulletin board."

He was referring to the notification of a Graduate Research Assistantship on one of the bulletin boards in the forestry building at the University of Idaho. I removed it from the board, took it to my undergraduate adviser, and asked Professor Leon F. Neuenschwander if he thought I was fit for graduate school. Dr. Neuenschwander tossed the flier onto his desk, asked a few questions, and then called his former graduate adviser on the telephone. A short conversation later, I was committed to pursuing my M.S. and Ph.D. at Texas Tech University with renowned fire ecologist Professor Henry

A. Wright. I started my academic career three months after removing the flier from the bulletin board.

From that simple beginning to the improbable task of writing about the horrors ahead, with abundant accolades along the academic way, here I am. Blessed -- or cursed -- with the eyes to see where I am and a brain to wonder why I landed in the "third" world as a result of (1) a privileged, tortuous path littered with myriad seemingly incidental turns on the proverbial road, and (2) a meteor striking Earth a couple hundred miles north of where I lived in Belize. We all came into being as a direct result of that same interstellar object igniting the oil fields that dimmed the planet sufficiently to cause the extinction of the dinosaurs and the consequent proliferation of mammals.

Along the way, and consistent with my written prediction as I graduated from high school in 1978, I became known for McPherson's Paradox and McPherson's Rule. The prediction, which I recently rediscovered: "I will discover a mathematical rule known as McPherson's Rule." The match is not exact, but it is surprisingly close.

McPherson's Paradox, coined by an online supporter: Civilization is a heat engine and turning off civilization heats the planet even faster. This paradox is rooted in the knowledge of civilization as a heat engine, based on the Laws of Thermodynamics, as well as on the evidence underlying global dimming (i.e., the aerosol masking effect).

McPherson's Rule, named by yours truly as a joke: Murphy was an optimist. This rule acknowledges Murphy's Law that states that, "Anything that can go wrong, will go wrong." I employ gallows humor to conclude the worst-case scenario is actually optimistic compared to our individual and collective near futures.

It has been quite a run. Through all the character defamation, libel, slander, and attempted assassination tossed my way, I have remained steadfast in my principles and also in my dark sense of humor. I am nearly done. Ever attempting to remain detached from the outcome, I am nonetheless satisfied with the choices I have made.

And, yes, it has been quite a run. Through all the challenges thrown in the path of humanity, some among us remain capable of decency. We are nearly done. For better *and* worse, from honor to horrors, we have left our mark on the third rock from a cosmically insignificant star.

It is time to let go, yet again. It is time to move on, yet again. For me, and for us.

## *Is Mine a Spiritual Message?*

I am frequently accused of, or credited with, presenting a spiritual message. The statements typically emanate from people I am inclined to describe as spiritually religious. I used to argue with them. I no longer argue, and my message has not changed. I have.

I am a rationalist. I have no place in my life for paranormal or supernatural phenomena. I generally describe myself as either an indifferent agnostic or a militant anti-theist. My perspective on rationalism has not wavered in the many years since I have concluded abrupt climate change will lead to near-term human extinction. Yet, I have changed.

I am more compassionate than I was all those years ago. I am kinder, too, and more tolerant. Yet these are not the attributes to which I refer when I mention I have changed. Rather, a definition and an etymology come into play, as I turn again to my dictionary.

Spiritual (initial definition): of, relating to, consisting of, or affecting the spirit: *incorporeal spiritual* needs.

Digging deeper, into the etymology, we find that spirit is derived from the Latin root *spiritus,* literally, breath, from *spirare* to blow, breathe.

American poet Charles Bukowski famously pointed out: "We're all going to die, all of us, what a circus! That alone should make us love each other but it doesn't. We are terrorized and flattened by trivialities, we are eaten up by nothing."

Am I spiritual? I certainly do not believe in ensoulment, an idea for which there is no evidence. I do not believe in god(s). In fact, I used to tell my students, most of whom were pursuing one of the Abrahamic religions, that I believed in one fewer god than they did. I would occasionally mention the 33 trillion Hindu gods, much to the surprise of my students.

I used to rabidly deny any religious spirituality. I still do.

Am I spiritual? I believe breathing is important. I believe how we breathe affects our thoughts. I believe the movement of air -- that is, the wind -- impacts everything from the structure and function of ecosystems to our daily emotions. Without wind of a certain direction and speed, our food supply declines profoundly and perhaps even vanishes.

I am a fan of food. Does that make me spiritual?

Was Bukowski's message a spiritual one? I suspect your answer to that question is the same as your response to the question about my spirituality.

# Chapter 5: Only Love Remains

*Truth is everybody is going to hurt you: you just gotta find the ones worth suffering for*


## (Bob Marley)


I am often incorrectly accused of "giving up" the patriarchal battle to "fix" climate change by promoting only love. There are many faults with this accusation, including the notion of giving up, reversing an abrupt and irreversible trend, and the laser-like focus on a single emotion. These are hardly the only false accusations tossed my way. I will tackle these three within the initial few paragraphs of this chapter.

Where to begin? I start with the long-running joke of my giving up. I gave up everything except my integrity -- including all money, prestige, and relationships -- to try to stop the planetary destruction resulting from civilization. In return, some people claim they have given a few dollars to wage the battle against climate change. As if the adherence to a monetary system driving us to extinction will stop or slow the process of extinction.

Item Two is reversing the irreversible. We are in the midst of abrupt, irreversible climate change. Within a culture in which celebrity is valued over science, opinion is valued over fact, and authority is valued over evidence, abrupt is confused with gradual and irreversible is assumed to mean "If we just try hard enough, we can turn this trend around." Human hubris knows no bounds.

Item Three takes us from the ridiculous to the sublime. From a friend comes this comment about love: "I think that perhaps love does not remain because it is a silly concept and a failure to articulate something more clearly." He goes on to write, "Love is nothing more than a trick we play on ourselves and a hegemonic device."

My cryptic response: "All emotions might be similar tricks, although I doubt it. I suppose it depends upon definitions, as usual."

I left it there with him. I continue the conversation here, beginning with a definition. The online Merriam-Webster Dictionary's first definition of love is, "strong affection for another arising out of kinship or personal ties."

Due to a lifetime of kinship and personal ties, I love the living planet. The concept is abstract to most people, which precludes their understanding. The concept is pragmatic and also concrete for me, which allows the relationship to have meaning. The meaning is not explicable to those unable or unwilling to develop a loving relationship with the living planet.

Even rudimentary understanding is beyond most people embedded within a culture that refers to relationships as resources. When the living planet is accepted as a collection of resources, there is no love.

I have never suggested love could make a dent in the climate-change predicament. I have pointed out that sometimes predicaments do not have solutions, and trolls lacking linguistic skills remain unimpressed. I am still not suggesting love can make a dent in the climate-change predicament. I am suggesting it can make a difference in the lives of most people.

Love is worth experiencing pain, at least for me. Love is worth suffering for, at least for me. Love is worth dying for, at least for me. No definitions are needed for this kind of love. Not for me.

## Two Examples

Not so long ago, a friend and neighbor mentioned my courage. In a discussion about the homestead I created in New Mexico, he said, "You were brave to do that with other people."

I was taken aback by this comment. At the property in New Mexico that I called the mud hut, I simply did what I have always done: I threw myself into a project. I assumed I would get back what I put into the project, if not more, as has generally been the case during my privileged life.

In retrospect, I understand my neighbor is correct. An act that made perfect sense when I was idealistic about people seems utterly ridiculous in the rear-view mirror. Absent my contemporary cynicism, my love for humanity more than a decade ago was a hallmark of my naive, inspired life.

We will do almost anything for love. We will leave our jobs. We will forsake power, money, and relationships in its name.

And so I have.

Idealism is expensive. It costs money and time. Perhaps most importantly, at least to me, it costs health. I do not mean merely physical health either, although I am clearly not the vibrant, young man I was several years ago: Mental, psychological, and emotional health are placed at great risk when one depends upon others in a culture gone mad.

As a symptom of cultural madness, nearly everybody within the mainstream culture treats greed as a god. It is the only god of significance to most people, platitudes to the contrary notwithstanding.

Christianity's golden calf is manifest daily in the form of myriad examples diametrically opposed to religious ideals.

Theft has become normal. Murder, too. We ignore them, paid off with the crumbs of this oligarchic empire.

"At least I'm not being robbed." Perhaps not yet. Not today. Not obviously, at least to you.

"Only terrorists are dying from NATO's bombs."

"We live in a democratic society." Wrong again.

"I did not vote for this." Except by thousands of actions, that is.

Any existential port in a shitstorm. We are sadly living out the words American science fiction writer Robert Heinlein penned years ago: "Man is not a rational animal; he is a rationalizing animal."

Afraid to push back -- after all, we are "safe"-- most of us abandon every principle for a few dollars and a little security. Is it any wonder we have given up virtually every aspect of personal freedom in exchange for virtual lives? Sowing and reaping are separated only by time. Time is always short.

I have often been told to follow my heart. I am not sure of the full meaning of this common expression, although I suspect it means surrendering intellect for emotion, which does not seem like a great idea. Dominated by the left hemisphere of my brain, I am reluctant to pursue such a path. On the rare occasion I have shifted the reins from the left hemisphere of my brain to my right, the outcome has been unpleasant. Perhaps I need more practice.

There are two exceptions to the generally undesirable outcomes resulting from my emotive decisions: my partner of more than 35 years, my spouse for more than three decades. She supported me throughout my mistake-ridden path, absorbing the frequent shocks along a road riddled with potholes. I was never worthy of her, and she certainly deserved better than me. May she find it. The universe is unjust, along with most of its participants. The second exception is my current partner, the one who owns the property in Belize where many of these words were typed.

The courage identified by my friend and neighbor is authentic, to the extent authenticity is meaningful. It is part of who I am, or at least who I was. Yet courage pales in comparison to the valor demonstrated by my loving partners.

## *Living on the Edge*

I read John H. F. Shattuck's Freedom on Fire: Human Rights Wars and America's Response shortly after the book was published in 2003. The author had been Assistant Secretary of State for Democracy, Human Rights, and Labor during the administration of Bill Clinton. The following line, attributed by Shattuck to an unidentified United Nations peacekeeper in the Balkans, has been stuck in my head since I read the book: "If you're not living on the edge, you're taking up too much space."

I grew up in a small, redneck, backwoods logging town in northern Idaho. Weippe was home to 713 humans, according to the never-changing signs alongside the road marking each edge of town. It was also home to three large sawmills. It was big-timber country during the final years of the age of extraction. I returned to Weippe in 2017 to find the human population and the number of sawmills profoundly reduced in number.

Ten years after my birth, walking in the early morning to elementary school, I looked up to see a 13-year-old schoolmate pointing a rifle at my head. I knew better than to run. He would have been inclined to answer my fear with a bullet. I kept walking. It was not extraordinary. I did not bother to tell my parents for decades. It just never came up.

We were free-range children, consistent with the times. We played until dark, which came late during northern-Idaho summers. We bicycled for miles each summer day, we invented games, we fished nearby streams and rivers, and we were unconcerned with personal safety.

It was a rough, privileged life.

On a summer day in 1976, at the age of 16 years, I drove my parents' red-and-white 1971 Ford pickup truck 30 miles to the east bank of the Clearwater River near Greer. My younger sister and a couple friends joined me in diving into the strong, cold current. After a round of swimming and lounging on the rocks, my sister's best friend dove in again, only to be swept away. I lost my first contact lens when I swam to her and dragged her to safety.

My family moved from the Idaho village of Weippe to the Idaho village of Craigmont between my junior and senior years in high school. Across the Clearwater River, we went from the Weippe prairie to the Camus prairie, from a small drinking town with a timber-extraction problem to a smaller community dominated by growers of wheat and the supporting infrastructure.

Not long after the move from Timberburg to Farmville, I hosted a visit by my favorite receiver from a year earlier, when I quarterbacked the high school football team. Mark also happened to be my sister's ex-boyfriend. We were joined by my new favorite receiver, who happened to be my sister's current boyfriend. Apparently, I was inclined to throw the pigskin in the direction of my sister's boyfriends. Or perhaps she liked receivers. In any event, the three of us were hunting ducks in the aforementioned red-and-white pickup truck.

As with my contemporaries, I was embedded within gun culture. I doubt I would have minded the experience, even if I had been aware it was unusual.

Less than a mile from town, Mark started testing the action on my dad's Ruger Bearcat .22 pistol from the middle of the bench seat. Jim was resting the butt of his 12-gauge shotgun on the floor, the barrel jammed into his right shoulder leaning against the passenger door. He was 16, old enough to know better, and I had expressed my concern regarding the business end of his weapon on previous hunting excursions. My sister was his girlfriend, so there was no reason for me to nag him. We chatted about football and deer.

Only five miles down the road, still on the paved highway, the deafening report of a fired gun filled the cab of the pickup. I casually asked Mark why he found it necessary to trigger a round inside the truck. He proclaimed his innocence and we turned our questioning eyes onto Jim, whose saucer-like eyes and stunningly pale face suggested the worst regarding the shotgun jammed into his right shoulder.

Good news: Jim had moved the barrel below his shoulder. A few pieces of lead shot grazed his ribcage. More good news: All the shot missed the gas tank behind the seat.

Bad news: Dad would surely notice the hole in the Ford as well as the pieces of lead in the ceiling of the camper that was ensconced in the bed of the truck. More bad news: Only two hours stood between me and dark-thirty when I was expected back home.

Upon our arrival home, Jim leaped from the truck and walked to his family home without a goodbye. Mark vanished into the basement, leaving me to explain the story to my folks.

"Dad, we shot your pickup," I said feebly. I contemplated a joke about my infamy as a poor shooter, but thought better of telling him we shot it from the only place we could hit it: from inside the cab.

My folks, concerned primarily with our safety, did not express anger. As a bonus, I learned how to perform rudimentary bodywork and also how to paint the patched metal on the truck. Nobody except the beloved Ford was ever in serious danger.

That same autumn during my seventeenth year found me with three friends late one night on a railroad trestle towering over Lawyer's Canyon. My male counterpart told me the new kids in town showed their mettle with a touch of the nose on the white, wooden post marking the dividing line between two counties: Lewis County and Idaho County. The post teetered beyond a curve in the center of the trestle. It was tenuously held in place between two six-foot pieces of flatiron separated by four inches of air.

Assuming my new friend Michael would not lie -- one of many times I have made that error about people I believed were my friends -- I balanced on the two pieces of flatiron, walked the six creaky feet to the post, and touched my nose on a thin layer of peeling white paint. Too afraid to spin around, I walked backward to safety. I was greeted by Michael's face, drained of blood, and his shaky voice questioning my sanity.

I am surprised any of us survive our teen years. At least in my case, based on my chronically poor judgment, survival was unwarranted. Little did I know my near-death experiences were merely warmup acts for a life on the edge.

Whitewater rafting became a part-time passion during the five summers I served on a wildland firefighting crew. I donated little blood and no broken bones to the Clearwater River during dozens of heart-pounding excursions.

The wildfire protection area for the Craig Mountain helitack crew covered a million acres and included the Salmon and Snake Rivers, two of the deepest, steepest canyons on Earth. The camaraderie of the helitack crew was enhanced by the risk-taking Vietnam-vet helicopter pilot. He let us choose the music as we flew to the fire. He would occasionally stretch safety standards by allowing us to jump downhill from the ship as he hovered with the uphill skid on the sloping terrain of a steep canyon. He did not want us to waste energy walking a mile or two from the nearest safe landing spot.

A few years later, in graduate school, I was responsible for lighting prescribed fires up to 20,000 acres in size. Helicopters came into play again. As with my days as a 19-year-old, I was responsible for large numbers of humans and expensive equipment. Five seasons fighting fires led to five seasons of lighting fires. As a fireman willing to take risks, I once sprinted through a sheet of flames forty feet high, my face tucked into my inner left bicep and forearm. The error in judgment easily could have been fatal.

Skydiving came in my later years, after I was occupying an intellectually "safe" position as a tenured professor. A friend wanted companionship when she jumped from a perfectly sound fixed-wing aircraft. It seemed like a fine idea at the time. It still does, although I have not repeated the experience for about 15 years.

I've long been fearlessly challenging the intellectual and cultural envelopes into which I was born. I am still attempting to break out of the cell into which I was inculcated. I suspect mine is a terminal, irreversible condition.

I drove through Mexico to live in Belize, a long-time goal at the end of a charmed life. I am often informed this is a dangerous place. I did not notice.

Pursuing power clearly pays better than adherence to principle. The latter often proves fatal for careers and lives. Adhering to principle produces only one certain reward, the only meritorious validation: the ability to look in the mirror without embarrassment. It has been worth the price, so far.

Life is short. Fear and hope are nonsensical, four-letter words. Let go or be dragged.

According to Homer's Iliad, written more than 2,500 years ago: "Any moment might be our last. Everything is more beautiful because we are doomed. You will never be lovelier than you are now. We will never be here again." My life's experience validates Homer's observations.

# A Charmed Life

Walter Winchell was an American newspaper and radio gossip commentator credited with the expression I have heard thousands of times: "Love it or leave it." For nearly three decades, I chose the honorable third way: I tried to improve the culture in the country of my birth, the United States. I realized more than a decade ago the hopelessness of improving an irredeemably, irreversibly corrupt culture. I planned my escape.

The escape did not pan out. Compromise led me to the wilds in the financially poor state of New Mexico. It was the best I could do, for several years. I gave it my best, for several years. In short, I gave it my all, and I lost it all, at least essentially all that mattered to me.

I moved in July, 2016 from the homestead in New Mexico, which I call the mud hut, to the Central

American country of Belize. My 2003 Saturn Vue was part of a small caravan along the eastern coast of Mexico. I doubt I would have been as kind to a wealthy-looking Caucasian man from America as the young Mexican men with rifles I met along the way. I appreciate their good humor and patience, as my inability to speak Spanish interfered with our communications.

I lived for 27 months on a 57-acre property I sometimes refer to as Homestead 2.0. In short, I moved from a rock-pile in the desert to a rock outcrop in the jungle. I moved from a location likely to lose habitat for humans very soon to an area likely to lose habitat for humans even sooner.

According to uninformed trolls posting online under various aliases, I moved for a combination of three reasons: (1) to extend my life, (2) money, and (3) pussy. No, really. People actually write these things. There might be other stories. I am not sufficiently interested to keep track. I will nonetheless address each of the three primary misconceptions about my departure after a bit of an introduction.

None of this is anybody's business but my own, although I have always treated my life as an open book. Now that I am a minor public figure -- with an emphasis on minor -- I feel compelled to respond to the insanity I attract. Apparently, I am flypaper for freaks who seek any opportunity to shoot the messenger (figuratively, so far).

Particularly uninteresting are the people who are unwilling to differentiate the person from his or her work, as I opined above. The culture of celebrity continues to hold sway over an audience largely incapable of critical thought. Throughout an entire career in the academy, I tried to overcome an insurmountable wall of human stupidity. Clearly, I failed.

Back to the three points from above. During previous Mass Extinction events associated with rises in global-average temperature, the poles harbored life longest. Were I interested in maximizing the length of my time on Earth, I would move south. way south, to Tasmania, New Zealand, southern South America, or South Africa. I have received offers from each location, along with every continent on Earth except Antarctica. No, thanks. I am interested in maximizing the life in my years, not the number of years in my life.

So much for living a long time. What about material riches, the driving force behind many lives, perhaps most of them, in this culture?

The women with whom I spend most of my time these days are not wealthy. My beloved former long-time partner and spouse has access to more cash than all of them. She also has a job for which she receives a decent salary, an achievement out of reach for people promoting my work during the age of economic contraction. I am not strongly motivated by money, as is clear from my decision to opt out of a high-pay, no-work tenured faculty position at the apex of American Empire several years ago. Were I driven to accumulate material possessions, I would have made different choices about how and with whom I live.

As nearly as I can tell, and strictly as an unrelated tangent, marriage is a product of civilization. As with many such products, marriage produces great financial wealth for a few at the expense of many. I am not suggesting it will happen, but if marriage were outlawed, only outlaws would have in-laws.

Finally, let us turn to the most tawdry topic, one of many subjects rarely discussed within this culture: sex. I am a huge fan. However, sex does not have the same appeal it did when I was in my twenties, and I am a professional. Furthermore, it is only sex. We have been doing it a while, as a species. Look where it got us.

As indicated above, I am a professional, even though I do not get paid. I strive to achieve high professional standards including continued motivation by evidence rather than pleasures of the flesh.

Finally, with little time remaining in my life, I took action in response to the disparaging advice launched my way since I wrote my initial piece of social criticism. I left the USA, as I suspect Walter Winchell would have recommended. After all, he was notorious for trying to destroy the lives of the people he disliked. Among his favorite tactics were allegations of having ties to Communist organizations and accusations of sexual impropriety. In other words, he preferred smear tactics to evidence, much like my detractors.

I spent 27 months in Central America before returning to the country of my birth in October of 2018 to support my partner as she supports her family. I will likely continue my ongoing misadventures and I will continue to shine a light on them. If I am unable to leave my readers laughing in self-defense, as I suspect, then I will try to play Court Jester.

I formed a few impressions during my time in Belize, which I will share. In addition, this chapter responds to questions generated by my previous writing.

I am capable of critical thought and I am not paranoid (even if I were, I would still have enemies). It is clear to me, based on ample evidence, that my departure from university life was engendered by the dark underbelly of the United States known variably as the Deep State, the Surveillance/Security State, and the Central Intelligence Agency. I left my paid position under my own power. The Deep State undoubtedly worked with members of the university administration to reduce my ability to pursue my passion, which therefore encouraged and accelerated my departure. The administrators likely did not know they were being manipulated. My radicalism, particularly with respect to the modeling and promotion of anarchism, made me a target of the federal government. As one consequence, I will never be able to work for pay again doing the work I love. Not in the country of my birth and, because the Deep State has extensive tentacles, not on planet Earth.

Let us go back a bit. The ancient philosophers have inspired and radicalized me. They were instrumental in shaping my path. Signs of my radicalism were apparent in my teen years. Nonetheless, as with most people in this culture, I was largely lost, philosophically, through my teen years and beyond. Then

I discovered the ancients. I read, studied, pondered, and ultimately found myself via the ancients. When I write about "finding myself," I am referring to my existential anchor. I became comfortable in my own skin. In my experience, few people are capable of achieving such comfort. I also threw off some of the shackles of culture, including those involving "unmentionable" topics such as money, death, sex, and bodily functions. For example, I realized that money is no indicator of success, and celebrity status in a society that values money over life is no path to personal comfort.

I am a scientist and a teacher. I know my work does not appeal to irrational people uninterested in learning. The evidence regarding our near-term demise is clear, and fearful people, paid trolls, mainstream media personalities, ignoramuses, and idiots will continue to project animus as they operate in an evidence-free zone. I cannot control this behavior, nor will I try.

I will continue my unpaid work as long as I am able. Belize was hardly the ideal location from which to continue my work, primarily because of the terrible telecommunications infrastructure. I made it work for as long as my partner desired, and then I moved back to the United States. Belize is a wonderful place to live and it is also a nice place to partake of the discussion few are willing to have about near-term human extinction. I worked daily as part of an active homestead, as with my several years at the homestead I created in southern New Mexico.

The native people in Belize are financially poor due to manipulation of the economy. They work to live, the exact opposite approach pursued so long by me and many other people in the "first" world. In my limited experience so far, they are universally strong, tough, compassionate, and sweet. I am sure there are exceptions. I did not seek them out. To a great extent, a person gets what s/he gives.

In sharp contrast to the typical Belizean are the typical former friends, co-workers, and colleagues of mine. The latter people have concluded I was manipulated by sex and money to move out of the United States. As with most folks within a culture gone mad, they are motivated by power, as exemplified by money, and therefore cannot imagine I would move for other reasons. Love and empathy are in short supply and certainly do not make the conventional list of legitimate reasons to relocate.

Meanwhile, the woman who generously allowed me to occupy her property in the Maya Mountains often heard that I fear-mongered her into moving to that location. Apparently, neither of us is capable of a single independent thought, since we have both moved to Belize against our wishes. Fortunately for us, misery loves company -- especially miserable company -- which left us loving the pathetic company of ourselves and the downtrodden Belizeans.

That last sentence was an attempt at levity. It is clearly necessary for me to point out the joke every time, lest my mean-spirited detractors turn the joke on me.

Belize is hot, humid, and beautiful. The flora and fauna were excitingly new to me. The natives, particularly in the nearby Mayan village where I spent much of my time, are wonderfully attuned to nature's bounty. They know the seasons and the response of ecosystems to the seasons. They know which plants will alleviate which pains. They know life is short. They act accordingly. Now back in the country of my birth, I am trying to follow their lead.

In the spirit of throwing off cultural shackles, I continue to ponder my own death as a means of living with urgency. The fact that my body is covered with insect bites encourages my thinking about death via Zika, dengue, and malaria. If I have a choice, which seems unlikely, I will have my body envelope torn merely to break another taboo on my way out. I would rather die between a jaguar's jaws than from a mundane, albeit toxic blend of bugginess.

My days in Belize are behind me now, with the exception of visits as allowed by the continued persistence of industrial civilization. My long-time practices as a learner and a teacher continue to extend far beyond the humble, rented apartment I currently occupy.

## Charmed at Two Levels

Harvard evolutionary biologist Stephen Jay Gould named his book Wonderful Life for the film starring Jimmy Stewart. The text includes a line that captures the human experience: "May our poor and improbable species find joy in its new-found fragility and good fortune!" The book's title and this quote refer to the spectacular odds against Homo sapiens ever appearing on the planetary stage. The improbable, arbitrary events leading to our speciation and continued persistence are truly remarkable.

Humans never evolved to survive past 30 years or so. Individuals died from such inconveniences as disease, famine, and tooth abscesses. Our brains remain Neolithic and apparently are running at less than 10% of capacity. Cultural evolution outstrips natural selection even as our gravest problems are rooted in an ever-changing multicultural civilization always on the brink of its own demise. We have ground the living planet into dust in pursuit of greed and longevity. The goal: continued opulence. The outcome: near-term extinction. The customary response: surprise. After all, we consider ourselves supremely special.

With respect to odds and accidents with our species, so too with individuals. I frequently quote evolutionary biologist Richard Dawkins with respect to the improbability of DNA coming together to comprise the bag of water we call ourselves: "In the teeth of these stupefying odds it is you and I that are privileged to be here, privileged with eyes to see where we are and brains to wonder why."

Obviously, I concur. The same sentiments apply to my life, too. If you are averse to self-indulgent stories by me, about me, you will do well to stop reading now.

I was born into the captivity of civilization, although I failed to see the bars on the cage for several years. Stories from my early years had my parents longing for the day they would earn $6,000 per year. We would have it made!

I was fortunate to be born in 1960 during an age of economic expansion in the United States. The privileges I have enjoyed as a Caucasian man are truly astonishing and largely undeserved. As I have pointed out a few times in previous works, people who look a lot like me accrue privileges like horse dung collects flies.

I tried to die a few more times than mentioned above. I keep trying, according to people I encounter along the way. My continued survival certainly is only marginally my own fault, considering the mistakes I have made. Then again, I am amazed so many people survive their teen years.

As expected for an American in the 1960s and 1970s, I went to a small school in a small town where I was a respected scholar and athlete. As expected, I went to college, where I was bored and spent most of my time having fun. Failing to see other options, I reluctantly went to graduate school, where I excelled and continued to have fun.

College expenses were paid by scholarships and summers on a helitack crew. Graduate school meant lighting prescribed fires rather than suppressing wildfires. Today's blazes are intellectual, and much hotter than the earlier ones. Water and dirt doused the actual fires.

Reason, regardless of how strong, is ineffective on contemporary cauldrons rooted in denial.

Shortly after receiving my Ph.D., I grabbed the brass ring offered to me. Faster than expected, I became a professor at the age of 28 years. The "faster than expected" trend continued through associate professor and full professor status.

My career was unexpectedly meteoric, partly because I was talented and able to identify and exploit my talents. Primarily, however, if I were to hazard a guess, I was rapidly successful because I am a Caucasian man.

During my early days in graduate school, I married a wonderful woman. We were both 23 years old. Twenty-six years later, I willingly left the job I loved on the basis of principle and moved to the rural countryside. There I spent our hard-earned savings on a homestead. It thrived. I did not.

The principled move away from the apex of empire destroyed all my valued relationships, including those with family, friends, and colleagues. A primary goal underlying my move was to allow many more years together with my beloved partner, but more than three years at a distance irrevocably tore us apart. I had failed to attend to her happiness and therefore lost my own. She generously supported me and my work long after others denigrated both.

We were together for more than 35 years, far short of the forever we had in mind. In this culture, such longevity is hailed for its success. Why, then, has the pain of failure crept into my leaden heart?

Along the way, I have been kind to individuals, although not as kind as I would have liked. I am certainly not as kind as they would have liked. I have been patient, especially with people I barely know. My failure to change society's horrific course has haunted me through the years, as my inner teacher has overridden my Buddhist tendencies. Paradoxically, I have been simultaneously joyous and plagued by the contents of my mind.

I have demanded institutions do right, even when institutional representatives claimed doing right was too expensive or would set a bad precedent. Such unwavering commitment to principle is the primary reason I no longer work on campus. I have continued to observe the horrors of the industrial economy, commonly pointing out that the world is becoming a worse place every year, contrary to the perspective of my purposely ill-informed peers.

I am a witness. In bearing witness and reporting the horrors, I do not fit into the dominant culture.

My increasing radicalism turned me into a pariah. By the time I was 19 years old, I came to view awareness not as a gift, but as a curse.

I pursued excellence and insisted that my students do the same. As I told each of them, repeatedly, the correct choice is nearly always the most difficult path. Choosing right action is costly, and such decisions are generally punished by society. Penalties continue, many years later, for my own principled actions. I understand why most people choose to live and promote a life based upon lies.

If my former students are to be believed, I changed the lives of many of them, one life at a time. I learned from them, and they from me. Such a humble approach, including my teaching and modeling of anarchism in my classrooms, led to my early exit from university life.

I was influenced by the words of Edward Abbey, although I never met the man. Abbey, the "desert anarchist," influenced my work in the classroom, where I required each of my students to complete a significant piece of art or literature as a major part of their grades. Consider Cactus Ed's sentiments about the intersection of poetry and science: "Any good poet, in our age at least, must begin with the scientific view of the world; and any scientist worth listening to must be something of a poet, must possess the ability to communicate to the rest of us his sense of love and wonder at what his work discovers."

As a result of my integrative efforts, my science-minded peers denigrated my efforts in the classroom. I readily admit that my art, notably my simple writing, was and is worthy of insult. The writing itself rarely receives sufficient attention to attract the animus of critics, although the message is constantly under attack.

I long ago declared myself a court jester, somebody who would comfort the afflicted while the world burned. I am occasionally referred to as a "large child," and I assume the comment is a compliment.

Ultimately, I largely failed to accomplish my goals when I made the transition from academia to homesteading and then to the realm of public speaking. After I tossed away the brass ring, my income and quality of life spiraled down, at least as commonly measured. I discovered that, as the expression goes, freedom is not free. As with many artists, my adherence to principle led directly to poverty. Unlike my earliest years on Earth, this time I am aware of the poverty (and also the bars on the cell). The lack of money precludes activities I have long taken for granted, including eating well and driving short distances to visit friends.

I have been giving myself away so long, there is almost nothing left. A shadow of what I used to be, I miss what has disappeared. In the short time we are here, it is what we do that makes us who we are. I am not proud of numerous things I have done, although I am not ashamed of who I have become.

Given a non-existent choice, I am certain I would choose a different path. Giving up enormous privilege comes with enormous cost, and truth-teller is not an easy job. Upon reflection, it could have been better. It certainly could have been worse. ,

On the other hand, I am relatively free. Unshackled by the straitjacket of culture, I am never censored by institutions and rarely censored by myself. My words are virtually unfiltered by a culture gone terribly awry. I live where I want in a manner of my own choosing. In the historical sense, I pursue a life of leisure, as I did during my years on campus: I choose the work I do.

A relatively new concept, a product of civilization, money is not a worthy pursuit for any of us. It seems my disdain of fiat currency has led to a largely money-free existence, for better and for worse. So far, the going up is worth the coming down. Life has been good to me, so far.

# The Money Trap

I am frequently asked if I am worried about running out of money. Although I threw more than $2 million at a homestead I went on to sell for less than ten cents on the dollar, and although that leaves me with very little fiat currency, and although I am far too young to die from "natural" causes, I am not terribly worried about running short on money before I draw my last breath.

I try to keep in mind how I came into the world: struggling for air, and then crying. Covered in somebody else's blood, slapped on the ass by a stranger, with nothing to my name. Not even a name. It got worse from there. Then, because I chose wisely my time and place of birth -- not to mention my sex and race -- it got better. I started with nothing, and I still have most of it left. What's not to like?

For me, non-monetary issues are far more pressing than fiat currency. These are the "things" I fear will run short during my days on Earth. Though few of the items on my bucket list are things.

Foremost on my list is love. Few people can survive without love. I am not one of them. I live where I do for love. That love is manifest at several levels.

I loved being out of the United States, the country of my birth. Paradoxically, I moved back to the United States for love. I love life itself, which is obviously detested by nearly every consumer in the country of my birth. I love living, rather than making a living. I love a lifestyle counter to that found throughout or desired within most of the world: agrarian anarchy in Belize (vs. the disaster capitalism preferred in the country of my birth). There is more, of course, most of it even less worthy of mention in this slim volume than the preceding information.

After love comes a planet habitable for humans. Or maybe I have the first two issues reversed. There is no love without a habitable planet. For me, there is no point inhabiting a planet without love. Living without love is no life at all.

What else to do? I have plenty of advice for myself and others. Most falls under the category of love, broadly defined. Inspired by Stage 7 I described for Kübler-Ross's five stages of grief (Fuck It), my fuck-it list is considerably longer than my bucket list. My short list of advice follows, in no particular order: (1) Remain calm: Nothing is under control, (2) Pursue excellence, however defined, (3) Pursue love, as you define it, (4) Decommission nuclear facilities, (5) Be kind, beginning with yourself, and (6) Comfort the afflicted and afflict the comfortable, a task assigned to newspapers by Charles Fanning (and obviously ignored by the corporate, mainstream media).

Perhaps the remainder of this chapter will fill in some of the proverbial blanks.

## The Absurdity of Authenticity

I am often accused -- or credited, depending on one's perspective -- of leading an authentic life. As nearly as I can tell, the accusation or accolade refers to the following definition from Merriam and Webster: "true to one's own personality, spirit, or character."

Fundamentally, are we not all true to our personality, spirit, and character. How could we act otherwise, in the absence of multiple personalities? I have concluded that we have been captured by the culture in which we are immersed. We are unable to escape without killing ourselves, yet the culture is killing us.

We are some six millennia into the culture of Abrahamic religions. We are more than two millennia into western civilization and the six questions of Socrates: (1) What is good? (2) What is piety? (3) What is virtue? (4) What is courage? (5) What is moderation? (6) What is justice? Furthermore, every person reading these words is a product of an industrial civilization that depends upon the expansive use of fossil fuels.

Is this the only way to live? Is this the best way to live? Do our hyper-connected, high-tech lives lead us along paths of excellence, in the spirit of Socrates?

This culture is steeped in patriarchy and depends upon violence for its continuation. Is it safe to assume this culture is the ultimate expression of our humanity? Is it safe to assume that this culture is the best we can do simply because this culture is the only one we have known? Is it safe to assume there is no other way beyond the hierarchal set of living arrangements we have come to depend upon for money, water, food, and personal identity?

Questioning this culture and its underlying assumptions follows the model promoted and popularized by Socrates. Answering these questions requires one to step outside the normalcy bias and profound enculturation of the way we live. Asking challenging questions, much less answering them, requires enormous courage when the questions themselves refuse to validate, much less approve, this irredeemably corrupt system.

I do not claim to know the answers to these questions. Indeed, I am not certain they have answers independent of the person pondering them and his or her personal experiences. I nonetheless believe it is important to ask the questions and develop personal responses to them. As a result, I will tackle these and related questions in this chapter. For the most part, culture discourages us from asking, much less answering, most of these questions.


## *Questions, Questions, and More Questions*

Throughout our lives, we spend considerable time seeking feedback from people and institutions, but the feedback we seek generally falls within a small subset of important issues. Furthermore, I question the wisdom of seeking validation, much less approval, within the realm of an irredeemably corrupt system.

Some of us seek to conduct meaningful lives. However, the universe imposes upon us a meaningless existence. There is no meaning beyond the meaning(s) we create. In attempting to create meaning, which often involves attempts to outrun our mortality, we generate distractions. We occasionally call them objectives, goals, or acts of service to others. The result is our legacy.

Yet it is too late to leave a better world for future generations of humans. The concept of leaving a legacy becomes moot when staring into the abyss of near-term human extinction. What, then, is the point? Are we, in the words of English poet Frances Cornford in her poem, "Youth," "...magnificently unprepared for the long littleness of life"?

As we seek feedback about the conduct of our lives, we simultaneously seek distractions. The distractions include the movies we watch, the books we read, the trips we take, the discussions in which we engage. The line blurs between distractions and authentic work until we are defined by the combination. The totality becomes who we are. The nature of our distractions is what makes us human, in the sense of differentiating us from other primates. Non-human primates do not read books, much less discuss them. Such distractions do not enable our survival and in that sense are not "necessities" (cf. food, water, shelter). However, they are not necessarily "luxuries," either. Apparently, there are shades of existential gray.

## *Shades of Gray*

Shades of existential gray are evident in our pursuit of meaningful lives. How do we differentiate between necessity and luxury? How do we distinguish what we want from what we need? And are these distinctions important?

When I began the ongoing process of walking away from the horrors of industrial civilization, I felt I had no choice. My inner voice overrode outer culture. I have subsequently come to realize that most people born into this set of living arrangements are literally and figuratively incapable of making a similar choice. Distinguishing between needs and wants, between necessity and luxury, is hardly clear.

Occasionally, we turn to wise elders in our attempts to infuse our lives with meaning. Kurt Vonnegut often quoted one of his uncles, in response to the question about meaning, who said, "We are here to fart around." Kurt's son Mark, between the loony bin and Harvard Medical School, responded to the question, "Why are we here?" with the following comment: "We are here to help each other through this, whatever this is."

I love Mark Vonnegut's response, but it fails to acknowledge that service to others is important and it is a trap. Service to others is no longer virtuous when the entrapment includes self-inflicted harm (including emotional or psychological suffering).

As the Buddha pointed out more than two millennia ago, to live is to endure suffering. Do we have an obligation to minimize suffering? Does that obligation extend to our individual selves, as well as to other humans? Does it extend to non-human species?

German philosopher Arthur Schopenhauer famously defined happiness as "The alleviation of suffering," implying a temporary condition. The pursuit of happiness -- from Schopenhauer's perspective, the alleviation of suffering -- is a right guaranteed by the founding document of the United States, but I have no idea why it is guaranteed or if it stops at the alleviation of suffering. If the alleviation of suffering qualifies as happiness, then it seems wearing shoes that are two sizes too small is a great strategy for producing happiness, if only at the end of the day when the shoes are removed from one's feet.

If happiness goes beyond the alleviation of suffering, perhaps it includes joy. The notion of such an idea drags into the discussion the notion of documentation, hence measurement. How do we measure joy? Is it the same as the bliss produced by ignorance? How do we know when we have stumbled upon it? And if joy is meritorious, even at the expense of suffering by another, how do we balance the existential books?

Consider, for example, a single example for the Abrahamic religions (aka patriarchy): marriage. Do we have an obligation to minimize the pain when a monogamous relationship becomes personally painful, or even a matter of indifference (i.e., lacking daily joy)? Contemporary culture suggests we muddle through, in sickness and health, until death. Naturally, the ultimate personal endpoint solves the problem of suffering.

# Why Are We Here?

I am often asked, "Why are we here?" Occasionally I am asked, "Why am I here?" I will attempt to respond to both questions in this short chapter. Not surprisingly, my responses align with the paragraph below from Schopenhauer, one of my favorite philosophers:

> "Human life must be some kind of mistake. The truth of this will be sufficiently obvious if we only remember that man is a compound of needs and necessities hard to satisfy; and that even when they are satisfied, all he obtains is a state of painlessness, where nothing remains to him but abandonment to boredom. This is direct proof that existence has no real value in itself; for what is boredom but the feeling of the emptiness of life? If life — the craving for which is the very essence of our being — were possessed of any positive intrinsic value, there would be no such thing as boredom at all: mere existence would satisfy us in itself, and we should want for nothing."

With respect to the first question, the one involving us, the obvious response is, who is the "we" targeted in the question? I will assume, in this case, that the "we" in question is Homo sapiens. In that case, the response is easy, if one has sufficient understanding of evolutionary biology.

I went to graduate school in Lubbock, Texas. In the process of completing my graduate degrees, I spent a lot of time conducting field work. On dozens of occasions, I defecated in the savannas. On most of these occasions, considering my location, I attracted dung beetles. The dung beetles would fly toward me as I squatted, their size and wingspan making them drone like B-52s. I would bat them away, as well as I was able, and they would crash awkwardly into my head and torso. After I finished the task, I would watch the beetles as they formed my manure into balls a tad smaller than ping-pong balls and then rolled them away.

These tiny creatures thus solved a significant problem for human beings. As with carrion beetles, dung beetles saved humans from a lot of life-threatening diseases.

By now it is probably obvious that the answer to the question, "Why are we here?" is rooted in evolutionary biology. We are here to give dung beetles something to do. Dung beetles are here to protect us, thereby extending our lives. Without us, dung beetles will be SOL.

As a civilization, I believe there is another response to the question of our purpose. We are here, as a global society of clever beings, to model ridiculous behavior. In so doing, *we provide a galactic warning to other civilizations in the multiverse.*

The far-more-difficult question is, "Why am I here?" I suspect there are approximately 7.7 billion answers to this question.

For uber-wealthy Jeff Bezos, the answer is, "go to the moon."

For uber-wealthy Elon Musk, the answer is, "go to Mars."

For some more-extreme technophiles, the answer is, "go even further."

I wish nothing but good luck to Bezos, Musk, and like-minded technopians. Well, I wish them a pleasant trip, too.

Some individuals are here to give. In pursuing a life of service, I would put myself and few others in that group.

Some people are here to take. We all know examples of those Daniel Quinn referred to as "takers."

For most of us, I would suggest that the individual rationale for our temporary existence is, "live small, breathe the sweet air, and go slow." Or, as Marcus Aurelius pointed out: "When you arise in the morning, think of what a precious privilege it is to be alive -- to breathe, to think, to enjoy, to love." I would go a few steps further in pointing out that the answer has to do with acknowledging our limits, as individuals.

If you are not a fan of Aurelius, perhaps George Carlin is more your style: "A person of good intelligence and of sensitivity cannot exist in this society very long without having some anger about the inequality. It's not just a bleeding-heart, knee-jerk, liberal kind of a thing! It is just a normal human reaction to a nonsensical set of values where we have cinnamon flavored dental floss and there are people sleeping in the street."

My lifetime of privilege has me waking up every morning at 3 a.m., plus or minus 15 minutes. Every morning, since August of 1979, the terrors come. The forever-empty feeling in the pit of my stomach greets me. Perhaps you have it, too.

I awaken at other times, too, typically about every three hours. However, nothing matches the precision of my 3 o'clock internal alarm, regardless of the time zone I am visiting.

I know almost everything is beyond my ability to control. I know there are many things I cannot fix. Most of them are beyond fixing, whatever that means. The others are beyond my ability to fix, whatever that means. As with most people reading these words, I want to leave the world a better place than when I arrived here.

So far, my record is not that great. I was born into captivity as a first-world human. That right there is a tremendous burden to shoulder.

I have a lifetime of conspicuous consumption in my rear-view mirror. It is not pretty. I have "must go faster" ringing in my ears. I have Mother Culture whispering "success" and "money" in the same breath, yet I know better. I have known better since August of 1979.

What is one poor, conflicted, privileged, Caucasian man supposed to do about abrupt, irreversible climate change on a polluted planet? This is the nagging question. This is the never-ending, forever-empty feeling raging at my nonexistent soul at 3 o'clock every goddamned dark morning.

Enlightenment is a curse. How can I push it away? How can I switch off my relentless mind, when the problems and predicaments keep piling up?

Obviously, it was not abrupt, irreversible climate change nagging me in 1979. That is merely the latest cabal of demons haunting me in the early morning. However, too many humans fouling the nest on a planet we've made way too small has been on my mind for a very long time. The Club of Rome's Limits to Growth hit the streets when I was 12 years old. Our collective response -- demanding more, better, faster at every imaginable cost, forever -- has been working fine, so far, for some of us. To assuage our mental health, it is best not to think about those for whom it is not working out. After all, you surely cannot expect one poor, conflicted, privileged, middle-aged Caucasian man to fix everything.

What am I making better? Why am I here? What is my purpose? These are the questions emanating from the forever-empty feeling in the pit of my stomach.

# The Cost of Happiness

If happiness is a goal, and if that happiness extends beyond the mere alleviation of suffering, how do we evaluate happiness? If our own happiness comes at the expense of another, how do we justify our gain? Equally important, but rarely considered, is the converse question: If our suffering brings happiness to another, how do we justify the personal pain? Is our own suffering less important than that of another?

How do we minimize suffering? Is such a quest restricted to humans, or are other organisms included? What is the temporal frame of the quest? Does it extend beyond the moment, perhaps to months or years? Does it extend beyond the personal to include other individuals?

We could minimize suffering to humans and other animals by playing solitaire in the woods. However, even that seemingly humble act takes life. Tacking on the seemingly simple acquisition of water, food, clothing, and shelter for a single human being in the industrialized world brings horrific suffering to humans and other animals. Attending to the needs of the nearly 8 billion humans currently inhabiting Earth comes at tremendous cost to the water, soils, and non-human species on the planet. Contemplating the desires of an increasing number of people on an overpopulated globe is enough to drive a thinking person to despair.

There is nothing inherently wrong with pleasure, yet the Greek word for "pleasure" forms the root of the English word "hedonism." According to my pals

Merriam and Webster, hedonism propounds that pleasure or happiness is the sole or chief good in life. When stated in this manner, pleasure seems to have taken a step too far. Drawing the line between personal pleasure and hedonism is no mean feat. Less often considered is the line we draw between personal suffering and the attendant happiness of others.

Lest we take the latter step too far, we should remember that the idea of hedonism some 2,500 years ago, when Socrates was haunting the Mediterranean region, was a bit different from the idea today. Back then, humans comprised a tiny drop in the large bucket known as Earth. The quest for personal pleasure and happiness at that time would have essentially zero impact on the natural world relative to the impact of today's quest for gratification by more than 7.7 billion people on this ever-shrinking and depleted orb.

When my happiness requires the suffering of another, is my happiness warranted? When the pleasure of another requires my suffering, is the suffering warranted? Does failing to contemplate questions about our needs and desires commit us to nihilism? Does living within the Age of Industry, hence participating in untold horrors to humans and other organisms, violate the Socratic notion of good?

# What About Empire?

American Empire is merely the most lethal manifestation of industrial civilization, hence any civilization. Because this culture is inextricably interconnected with this civilization, I have concluded that contemporary culture is worthy of our individual and collective condemnation. Walking away from empire is necessary but insufficient to terminate this horrific culture.

As nearly as I can determine, maintaining American Empire -- or any empire, for that matter -- requires three fundamental elements: obedience at home, oppression abroad, and destruction of the living planet. Unpacking these three attributes seems a worthy exercise, even acknowledging Voltaire's observation: "It is dangerous to be right in matters on which the established authorities are wrong."

Obedience at home means capitulating to culture and the government. It means abandoning a culture of resistance in favor of the nanny state. It means allowing the government to control the people instead of the other way around. It means giving up responsibility for oneself and one's neighbors and expecting the government to deal with all issues. Considering the excellent record of the government in transferring wealth from the poor to the rich while promoting an economy rooted in war, I have no idea why the people with whom I interact are fans of this government.

Oppression abroad is obvious to anybody paying attention to American foreign policy during the last hundred years. The government of the United States of Absurdity extracts taxes from the citizenry to build the most lethal killing force in the history of the world. This military, supported by cultural messages and therefore most of the consumer-oriented citizenry, is then used to extract materials such as fossil fuels from other countries. The resulting "riches" enjoyed by Americans serve to pacify the masses, embolden the government, and enrich the corporations that exert strong influence over both the media and the government.

Destruction of the living planet is imperative if we are to support seven billion people on the planet, many of whom want "their" baubles. Are we not entitled to transport ourselves around the world, dine at fancy restaurants for a few hours' work at minimum wage, entertain ourselves with music and movies, and all the rest on an essentially limitless list? Where do the materials originate for each of these endeavors? Are we so filled with hubris that we believe driving dozens of species to extinction every day is our right? Do we lack the humility -- and even the conscience -- to treat non-human species with respect?

Each of these three broad elements serves a subset of humans at the expense of others. Although obedience to culture prevents us from being viewed as "odd" to our straitjacketed acquaintances, it also serves the oppressors. Giving up on radicalism -- i.e., getting to the root -- fails to serve our needs while lessening our humanity. It does nicely serve those who pull the levers of industry.

Perhaps it is time we heed the words of deceased American social critic Christopher Hitchens: "To be in opposition is not to be a nihilist. And there is no decent or charted way of making a living at it. It is something you are, and not something you do."

## *Imperialism Has Consequences*

The U.S. Constitution and Bill of Rights are bobbing along on the same waves as social justice and environmental protection, and are sold down the river by a nation addicted to growth for the sake of growth (the ideology of a cancer cell). Indeed, it seems very little matters to the typical American beyond economic growth. For that goal, most importantly, we need an uninterrupted supply of crude oil. We need the Carter Doctrine -- the world's oil belongs to us -- and an unhealthy dose of faux patriotism.

Our lives are imbued with faux patriotism. We are manipulated by the war-loving corporate media and the war-loving politicians that, unsurprisingly, are enriched by war. We support the troops that bring us the baubles we are convinced we deserve, and we rarely question the real, underlying costs of the baubles.

"Support the Troops." It's the rallying cry of an entire nation. It's the slogan pasted on many of the bumpers in the United States.

Supporting the troops is pledging your support for the empire. Supporting the troops supports the occupation of sovereign nations because might makes right. Supporting the troops supports the wanton murder of women and children throughout the world. Men, too, of course. Supporting the troops supports obedience at home and oppression abroad.

Supporting the troops throws away every ideal on which the United States allegedly is founded. Supporting the troops supports the ongoing destruction of the living planet in the name of economic growth. Supporting the troops, therefore, hastens our extinction in exchange for a few dollars. Supporting the troops means caving in to Woodrow Wilson's neo-liberal agenda, albeit cloaked as contemporary neo-conservatism (cf. hope and change). Supporting the troops trumpets power as freedom and fascism as democracy.

I am not suggesting the young people recruited into the military are at fault. Victims of civilization and a lifetime of cultural programming -- like me, and perhaps you -- they are looking for job security during a period of economic contraction. The entire process is working great for the oppressors pulling the levers of industry.

Perhaps most important, supporting the troops means giving up on resistance. Resistance is all we have, and all we have ever had. We say, "I'm mad as hell and I'm not going to take it anymore." (The previous line, of course, spoken by actor Peter Finch in the great film Network written by Paddy Chayefsky.) Sadly, we collectively gave up on resistance of any kind years ago.

We act as if America's cultural revolution never happened. We act as if we never questioned the dominant paradigm in an empire run amok as if we never experienced Woodstock and the Summer of Love, bra-burning hippies and war-torn teenagers, Rosa Parks, and the Cuyahoga River. We are right back in the 1950s, swimming in culture's mainstream instead of questioning, resisting, and protesting.

We have moved from the unquestioning automatons of Aldous Huxley and George Orwell to the firebrands of a radical counter-cultural worldview and back again. A generational sea change swept us from post-war "liberators" drunk on early 1950s propaganda to revolutionaries willing to take risks in defense of late 1960s ideals. The revolution gained steam through the 1970s but lost its way when the U.S. industrial economy hit the speed bump of domestic peak oil. The Carter Doctrine coupled with Ronald Reagan's soothing pack of lies was the perfect match to our middle-aged comfort, so we abandoned the noble ideals of earlier days for another dose of palliative propaganda. Three decades later, we have swallowed so much Soma we could not find a hint of revolution in Karl Marx's *Communist Manifesto.*

In short, the pillars of social justice and environmental protection rose from the cesspool of ignorance to become shining lights for an entire generation. Then we let them fall back into the swamp. The very notion that others matter -- much less that those others are worth fighting for -- has been relegated to the dustbin of history.

A line from Eugene Debs, five-time candidate of the Socialist party for U.S. president, comes to mind: "While there is a lower class I am in it, while there is a criminal element I am of it; while there is a soul in prison, I am not free."

I do not harbor any illusions about my freedom. I lived in Police State America for the first 55 years of my life, and also now. I live on Planet Easter Island at the whim of Police State America.

## Imperial Illusions

Ultimately, I wonder why any of us bothers trying to be a virtuous person. As Ernest Hemingway indicated: "The best people possess a feeling for beauty, the courage to take risks, the discipline to tell the truth, the capacity for sacrifice. Ironically, their virtues make them vulnerable; they are often wounded, sometimes destroyed."

Vulnerability is not so bad, although few knowingly bring on their own destruction. Instead, I suspect most humans -- even those who consider themselves virtuous -- actually benefit from and even promote contemporary culture, the problems with which are legion.

Do good people promote patriarchy? Do they pursue and promote the notions of marriage and monogamy even when knowing these ideas are steeped in the patriarchy of a culture gone seriously awry?

Marriage and monogamy are obligations of empire rather than outcomes of natural law. Instead of aiding and supporting imperialism, shall good people attempt to reduce or eliminate patriarchy, hence civilization, one act at a time?

When we recognize patriarchy and its impacts, where does that leave those of us pursuing authenticity? Indeed, attempting to conduct an authentic life in a culture dominated by patriarchy that engenders destruction is analogous to pursuing meaning in an uncaring universe. Does authenticity have meaning in such a universe? Is authenticity a desirable goal, if goals are merely cogs in the machine of a culture run amok? Is authenticity another stumbling block on the road to happiness? Is authenticity yet another piece of propaganda promoted by the thieves and liars pulling the levers of civilization to trap decent people into lives of service? Do we ultimately and perhaps unwittingly serve civilization, hence the destruction of all life on Earth, when attempting to serve humanity?

If a life of service is a trap, why step into the trap? In avoiding the trap are we embracing nihilism, "a viewpoint that traditional values and beliefs are unfounded and that existence is senseless and useless"? And, if so, does the embrace constitute a pact with the proverbial devil?

As individuals and a society, have we become so broken we cannot pursue the truth about ourselves and our culture? Have we become so marginalized, demoralized, and humiliated by this insane culture that we are no longer able to rise up against cultural insanity?

# Chapter 6: Dancing at the Edge

*If I can't dance, I don't want to be part of your revolution*

(Emma Goldman)

## *I Am Che*

I am Che.

Too pretentious? Please allow me an explanation, beginning with a quote from Che Guevara: "At the risk of seeming ridiculous let me say that the true revolutionary is guided by a great feeling of love."

I have been called Che. I have also been called the Gandhi of climate science. Ditto for Jesus. I was called, by a two-year-old unable to pronounce my name, God. Calling me Che does not seem so pretentious now, does it?

Like Che, I am a warrior. Those with less fortitude would have surrendered long ago to the cacophony of culture. As I wrote many years ago, "We need witnesses and warriors" on behalf of the living planet. The longer version comes from an online essay I wrote in November, 2013: "We need witnesses to the carnage. We need to document the crimes against humanity as well as the crimes against nature. We need to illustrate alternatives and then live them. We need warriors if the living planet is to survive industrial civilization."

Like Che, I love being outdoors. From childhood to a career in field biology, from a college degree in forestry to my homesteading life in full view of the world's first designated wilderness area, from the deserts of the American Southwest to the jungle of Belize where I lived for 27 months, and from the small village in northern Idaho where I grew up to the large village in New York where I now live, I am purposely immersed in the wild.

Like Che, I provide a voice for those who cannot speak. The oppressed are my brethren. In my case, these include non-human organisms.

Like Che, I seek social justice. Unlike Che -- based on my limited understanding of his perspective -- I have been connecting it to environmental protection for a long time.

Like Che, I am a prolific writer. My radicalization in my teens came later in my life than his radicalization came in his.

Like Che, I am profoundly anti-empire. Like Che, I target American Empire as the worst example in history.

Like Che, and many reading these pages, I think deeply. On many topics, I question the dominant culture and its narrative, a practice with little reward beyond a largess of hate mail.

Unlike Che, I do not brandish a rifle, nor do I ride a motorcycle. On both counts, I suspect I would be more effective if I followed his rebellious lead.

Unlike Che, for better and worse, I have not been killed yet. I have already outlived him by more than 15 years.

Unlike Che, as nearly as I am able to determine, I have not yet killed another human. Well, not directly. I am certain I have killed many people indirectly, simply because I was long ensconced within history's worst example of imperialism.

Like Che, I eat, drink, and otherwise participate in modern society. Ergo, I am a hypocrite and murderer.

You are Che, too. With a single breath, you inhale a single molecule that emanates from Che's last exhalation.

We are Che. Much as this culture promotes the opposite belief, we are connected in material ways.

## *I Am Bill Hicks*

I have been called Che, for better and worse. I am taking it upon myself in this comparative section to analyze my similarities with American comedian Bill Hicks. As Hicks said, and as I would like to believe about myself, "I left in love, in laughter, and in truth, and wherever truth, love, and laughter abide, I am there in spirit." And I do not even believe in spirits.

I share Hicks's vision of "saving the world" by eliminating fear from our individual lives. I do not share his perspectives on immortality or the infinite-growth paradigm. I am sure there are many other differences between us. In this brief missive, I will instead focus on our similarities.

My primary resemblance to Hicks, who was born in the early 1960s about two years after me, is in the realm of social criticism. Hicks used humor as his primary truth-telling, dominant-narrative-disrupting device. I use humor when my creative juices take me that way, but I am hardly in the same league as the inimitable Hicks. My attempts at stand-up tragedy are pathetic relative to Hicks's incomparable stand-up comedy.

My social criticism might not seem very loving, especially when it lacks humor. I suspect it never seems loving to those under the lens of my critique. Failure to differentiate between kindness and niceness sometimes leads one to take personally a message intended for others. In my experience, the receipt of brutal honesty is best done with introspection.

As with Hicks, my professional career began at a young age. I was not paid to perform at the age of 14, as he was, but my career began and ended at ages considered young within my chosen profession.

As with Hicks, I am not timid. He was masterful at speaking his mind. As a result, he was heavily censored by mainstream institutions. He did not censor himself in response. Neither do I.

As with Hicks, my views are supported by evidence and they are contrary to the views of people within a population purposely dumbed down and willfully ignorant. As with Hicks, I point out the absurdities in a culture characterized by absurdity. Consider the lengthy quote from Hicks I mentioned in Chapter 3 about the two drugs tolerated by Western civilization: caffeine and alcohol, respectively during the week and on weekends.

As with Hicks, I am often subject to personal attacks. A quote from Hicks is relevant, with my detractors in mind: "Here is my final point. About drugs, about alcohol, about pornography and smoking and everything else. What business is it of yours what I do, read, buy, see, say, think, who I fuck, what I take into my body -- as long as I do not harm another human being on this planet?"

As with Hicks, I freely speak my mind. As with Hicks, I am freer than most people in this culture. I have been off the culturally imposed treadmill for years.

As with Hicks, I love the country of my birth. As with Hicks, I detest the profoundly powerful minority pulling the strings of American Empire. As with Hicks, I am able to distinguish between a country and its people, and also between individuals and herds.

As with Hicks, I am routinely criticized for my work. As with Hicks, these critiques almost never include evidence.

Toward the end of his short life, Hicks worked very hard to transmit his message of love to as many people as possible. Perhaps this approach is familiar.

Obviously, I am not Bill Hicks, and not merely because our talents are dissimilar. However, his final weeks provide inspiration for me as I pursue excellence and love.

# I Am Here

When asked why we are here, the inimitable American author Kurt Vonnegut frequently quoted his son Mark as well as one of his uncles. The former individual, between stints in a psyche ward and Harvard Medical School -- and apparently those were two different facilities -- Mark Vonnegut answered, "We are here to help each other through this, whatever this is." According to Kurt Vonnegut, one of his uncles said, "We are here to fart around, and don't let anybody tell you any different."

I agree with both of Kurt Vonnegut's sources. Committed as I am to a life of service, I strongly support the perspective expressed so eloquently by Mark Vonnegut. At least for me, any other life is pointless. If I cannot serve humans and the rest of the living planet, then my life has no purpose.

Inspired as I am by the absurdist philosopher Camus, I cannot fault Kurt Vonnegut's uncle. When I am unable to have fun on a daily basis, including the ability to poke fun at the culture into which I was born, then it is time for me to go. For the many people who have recommended my early exit, the terminus of my fun-filled adventures will be a happy day. Even my death will bring giggles of joy. *That*, for me, epitomizes a service-filled life.

Recognizing that all is impermanent and still finding meanings in an amoral, meaningless universe have been guides along my path to a life replete with simple pleasures. Introspection has been pivotal at every turn.

Introspection, a synonym for the intrapersonal intelligence described by educator Howard Gardner as one of ten different kinds of intelligence, is a rare skill. As with Gardner's other categories, intrapersonal intelligence is innate and it can be improved. As Gardner skillfully points out, intrapersonal intelligence is ignored and disparaged in K-12 indoctrination facilities. Such is the case for all except two of Gardner's ten kinds of intelligence, logical/mathematical and linguistics.

In the absence of intrapersonal intelligence, hence the inability to ponder one's purpose in a confusing and complicated world, many people seek external validation and acceptance from a culture gone mad. This leads quite unnaturally to money as gawd and introspection as a waste of time and cognition. Thus are many people led to believe postmodern palaver such as truth is personal, with the obvious and obviously ludicrous conclusion that there are as many versions of the truth as there are people. Forsaking personal responsibility is a clear next step.

Dependence upon an irredeemably corrupt system is thereby strengthened.

Voila! The perfect storm of idiotic consumerism is created within a purposely dumbed-down society. The rich get richer. The poor become increasingly ignorant and stupid and insanely continue to support an insane set of living arrangements. One consequence: The lies my culture told me -- and still tell me -- gain additional traction every day.


## *Lies My Culture Told Me*

With a hat tip to inspired by James W. Loewen's popular 1995 book, *Lies My Teacher Told Me: Everything Your American History Textbook Got Wrong*, note my preferred pronunciation for this set of living arrangements: siv-uh-LIE-zey-shuhn. The entire phenomenon -- reminiscent of Nietzsche's "thing as it is" -- is a fraud. It is characterized by lies heaped upon deception. Individuals are rewarded for lying. Truth-tellers are punished. George Orwell had all this figured out in his 1949 book, *1984*: "The further a society drifts from truth the more it will hate those who speak it." And, as with the future depicted in some science-fiction films, there is no possibility of escape.

Examples are legion. I list below and briefly describe a few.

Throughout this short section, "we" refers to the civilized version of our favorite species, *Homo sapiens.*

We perceive ourselves as supreme in every way. What applies to other species, from this viewpoint, does not apply to humans. From the "Eastern" religions through the Abrahamic religions and all the way to humanism, humans are superior.

We can and will experience infinite growth on a finite planet. There are no limits to growth in any form, from the industrial economy to the human population. Notwithstanding abundant science and simple logic, we can grow forever.

More is better. This single, simple phrase is a decent definition of contemporary human society. More of what? Everything. Just more. That is all we want. That is all we need.

Everything, every *thing*, and every being must be monetized. From soil to oil, from water to air, from joys to toys, everything must be assigned value. What kind of value? The only kind this culture understands: the kind with dollar signs.

Thinking positive is the first step toward a better future. Hope, otherwise known as magical thinking, is unimpeachably good. To relinquish hope is to give up on humanity.

Racism is normal. Misogyny is normal. Poverty is normal. Identifying others as *others* is normal.

Monetary disparity is customary and expected. Poverty is customary and expected, even though it did not exist until money was created coincident with the first civilizations. Monetary disparity and poverty are the means by which we keep track of the winners and losers.

What could possibly go wrong? Probably nothing that hasn't already.

I am no longer playing that game. I have been describing the horrors of this culture for decades and actively attempting to distance myself from the "civilized" life for more than a decade. Notwithstanding my failed attempts to date, I continue to seek my life's meanings liberated from the shackles of a culture from which I cannot escape.

I am passionately pursuing a life of excellence even as I rediscover and reinvent what this means for me. As Vincent Van Gogh said, "I would rather die of passion than of boredom." Your mileage may vary. I have no doubt it does, considering the personal nature of excellence, meaning, and love.

I am here to learn. I am here to describe what I have learned.

I am here to live. I am here to love.

I am here, living in the here and now. Please join me.

# Two Letters

In the spirit of completing otherwise-incomplete relationships to overcome my grief, I have penned a letter to my past. And, in the spirit of offering explanations for our collective behavior, I have also penned a letter to the future. I doubt I will accomplish either goal. I am trying to remain unattached to outcomes.

# A Letter to My Past

Dear ex-friends, -colleagues, -coworkers, -family, and -students,

This letter attempts closure. Your incomplete relationship with Guy McPherson is comprised of ragged edges. This letter attempts to smooth some of the edges before we die.

Guy knows he's not the same person he used to be. He killed the Buddha years ago. The Guy McPherson you claim to know disappeared long ago. To kill the Buddha is to destroy one's identity.

The fully indoctrinated agent of imperialism who formerly promoted civilization became fully aware of the horrors of the "normal" set of living arrangements. The resulting, personal changes were rapid and dramatic. Too many of the changes turned out badly.

Change is the only universal constant. McPherson's changes, for better *and* worse, left him a profoundly different man than he had been a decade previously. Among these changes were the shattered core of his identity and a plethora of confused people in the wake. McPherson's quest for redemption began after the shattering was complete, too late to ameliorate the resultant confusion.

McPherson's personal pursuit of excellence had for years focused on freedom of expression, as exemplified during every session of each course he administered. Early in his career, he came to understand the words of Aeschylus, albeit from his perspective as an anti-theist: "He who learns must suffer, and, even in our sleep, pain that cannot forget falls drop by drop upon the heart, and in our own despair, against our will, comes wisdom to us by the awful grace of God." And yet, through the agony, Guy McPherson taught. Miraculously, a few learned as a result of his caring efforts.

Among the results of McPherson's teaching were receipt of the highest awards endowed by the only two transdisciplinary colleges at the University of Arizona (Graduate College in 2002, Honors College in 2009). That he was a great educator is indisputable. Years later, he admitted he could no longer achieve the same level of greatness in the academy, even were he given the opportunity, largely because his idealism had given way to cynicism. He no longer expected every person to exceed his high expectations. He had been set up and knocked down too many times for his faith in each individual to persist. Still, he refused to lower the bar for himself or others. No longer able to continue down the road of expectations into which he was born, he tried to escape.

McPherson's failure to change society's horrific course haunted him to his dying day. His inner teacher continued to override his Buddhist tendencies until the end. He would have benefitted had he paid closer attention to J. Krishnamurti at a young age: "It is no measure of health to be well adjusted to a profoundly sick society."

After abandoning the academy, McPherson rarely heard from the people who formerly dominated his life. The infrequent interactions were filled with tales of his insanity based upon a rare brain disease. Paradoxically, former students occasionally told him that, when encountering difficult decisions in their careers, they asked themselves, "What would Guy do?" It is difficult to imagine a higher form of flattery.

The official response to McPherson's increasing radicalism was harsh. He was disparaged, marginalized, and ultimately cast aside by a society that worships money over life, power over beauty, and war over love. He sought a new life, free from the shackles of empire. Filled with hope, he tried to lead the way out of planetary omnicide and extinction of life on Earth.

A line from *Mad Max: Fury Road* comes to mind. Near the end of the film, Max, played by Tom Hardy, speaks from personal experience: "Hope is a mistake. If you can't fix what's broken, you'll go insane."

McPherson could not fix what was broken. He lost hope and deemed the loss good. He lost his way, with mixed results. He lost his "civilized" mind. It cost him everything. Essentially every material possession. Every relationship he held dear.

Recognizing that the culture monetizes and therefore trivializes everything -- including every single thing and every being -- offered no consolation for his losses. Rather, it was a reminder about the haunting words from Aeschylus. Suffering and despair had become constant companions, intertwined with the wisdom he had acquired.

This undesirable outcome explains why so many prefer willful ignorance. As Adyashanti pointed out: "Enlightenment is a destructive process. It has nothing to do with becoming better or being happier. Enlightenment is the crumbling away of untruth. It's seeing through the facade of pretense. It's the complete eradication of everything we imagined to be true."

Soon after McPherson's attempted escape, he discovered the only escape is the final one, as elucidated by Homer in the *Illiad*: "The gods envy us. They envy us because we're mortal, because any moment may be our last. Everything is more beautiful because we're doomed. You will never be lovelier than you are now. We will never be here again."

McPherson came to welcome the moment the gods envied. Ceasing to exist became preferable to being fully present in the current moment. Picking through the remaining shards in search of meaning brought heartache. Lacking other options in the face of our near-term demise, he pursued the same goals toward which he encouraged others: excellence and love.

This message is not goodbye, although McPherson's weak will to live combines with his metropolitan location to ensure he will be among the first humans to join the myriad other beings we drive to extinction each day. You'll not be far behind, contrary to his wishes. He sends you his sincere good wishes during these fine, final days.

Sincerely,

Guy (version 2.0)

P.S. The postscript to an error-riddled past comes from American poet Charles Bukowski: "The problem was you had to keep choosing between one evil or another, and no matter what you chose, they sliced a little bit more off you, until there was nothing left. At the age of 25 most people were finished. A whole god-damned nation of assholes driving automobiles, eating, having babies, doing everything in the worst way possible, like voting for the presidential candidates who reminded them most of themselves.

I had no interests.
I had no interest in anything.
I had no idea how I was going to escape.

At least the others had some taste for life. They seemed to understand something that I didn't understand. Maybe I was lacking. It was possible. I often felt inferior. I just wanted to get away from them. But there was no place to go."

# A Letter to the Future

I have a few suggestions if you are interested. First, please accept an apology on behalf of my self-absorbed species. We left a tremendous mess. Sorry about that.

The mess is so bad, I am surprised you are here. We left a small world in our wake, populated with microbes, bacteria, fungi, and similar "simple" life forms.

You must have brought what you need to survive. Maybe several million turns around the sun have passed after the year we called 2019. Probably you are self-reliant *and* way too late to our little extinction party.

Earth's final civilization turned out great for a few people. Hot showers and bacon were the highlights for many of us. In retrospect, destroying our only home for a few bucks and a BLT was not the swiftest plan we could have developed. To the "credit" of our species, most people were too ignorant and too stupid to evaluate evidence, so perhaps only the small minority of us sounding the alarm are to blame.

Anyway, back to that unsolicited advice. I have little to say and I am hardly a reliable source. After all, my species went extinct at a young age. I predicted and documented our fall, but I did not prevent it. Too late, I realized the untoward behavior of the civilized members of my species could not be swayed by rational thinking.

If you are reading these words and comprehending their meaning, then it is too late for my premier bit of advice: Do not use written language. Yes, it is temptingly beautiful, like a flower with thorns or a venomous invertebrate. Nonetheless, using language, like using thorns or venom, is a short-term proposition. Death can result from a single contact from any of the three.

If you come across anything flammable, run away. Somebody in your group is bound to harness the fire, at least for a while. Shortly thereafter, you will all discover fire cannot be harnessed for long. This white-hot lesson will come after the exam.

Language and fire are the two major forces leading to the destruction of habitat. Without them, you will last long. With them, you will soon be gone. I suspect my warning is too late for either of the two.

Beyond language and fire, recognize that there are a few other factors that can contribute to your early demise. Civilization comes immediately to mind and, as with language and fire, I suspect I am too late. Civilization is nearly as tempting as language and fire.

Civilization, to be brief, means storing food. Once the food is stored, it becomes easy to keep from some people. So the food is locked up and ultimately assigned monetary value. A few blinks of the eyes later, you're all dead.

Contrary to one of the overriding messages of civilization, *there are no others.* If you contemplate idolizing, worshiping, insulting, or attacking others, throw yourself into a volcano before the idea catches on. The others you believe you see are, in fact, the various forms of you. Treat them -- and by them, I mean yourself -- as you would treat yourself, not like you treat the pocketknife you borrowed from your cousin. Treat them with dignity, respect, and love.

Remember that everybody dies and that all species go extinct. See. Smell. Taste. Listen. Touch. Breathe. Learn. You want more? Really? To what end, beyond a quick and violent end?

Like every living being, you have needs. Unlike many living beings, you also have desires that you are able to recognize. Learn to distinguish the needs from the wants and focus on securing the former. If you do not obsess about your desires, you will be happier. Notice that the beings that are not plagued with desires -- the reflections of yourself -- will persist a while longer. And so will you and those you care about.

Care more than you believe is possible. Wear your proverbial heart on your proverbial sleeve. Let it get smashed. Love, and suffer as a result. Trust me: It is all worth it. The going up is worth the coming down. The pain of living -- really living, not merely making a living -- is occasionally rewarded by joy.

I doubt you can find joy. If you are lucky and attentive, it might find you.

If joy finds you, revel. Embrace the moment. Remember it. You might even jot down a note. If ever you stumble across the opportunity to create the conditions that brought you joy, seize the moment on behalf of someone else. After all, that someone else is really another form of you, longing for a moment of joy to relieve his or her suffering. If you are given the rare privilege of creating joy for another, and you do not pursue it, please take advantage of that volcano mentioned above.

Finally, remember this: Moments matter. They are all you will ever have. They are gifts of enormous magnitude. Be grateful. Make them count.

## *The Quest for Joy*

What does it mean to be happy? The simple definition, according to my buddies Merriam and Webster, is "feeling pleasure and enjoyment."

What is required to feel pleasure and enjoyment? Sex, drugs, and insanity are the obvious choices. Depending on the individual, there are many more.

It seems to me that happiness is a relatively superficial condition. I am happy, or perhaps merely distracted from suffering, when I am having sex or smoking a certain herb. Such activities, at least by themselves, do not bring me joy.

I speak and write about taking a radical approach. A radical gets to the root. Radicalism assumes going deep.

Joy is a deeper experience than happiness. It requires more than scratching the emotional surface. In return, it offers an experience more fulfilling than happiness.

Then what about joy, according to Merriam and Webster? The simple definition claims joy is "a feeling of great happiness."

The difference between being happy and experiencing joy, according to Merriam and Webster, is minor. I would argue the difference is simultaneously minor and quite significant. Beyond the superficiality of happiness lies the much more meaningful emotion of joy.

No sex, drugs, or insanity are required for joy. I doubt they even help one make the transition from happiness to joy.

Upon reflection, I doubt I am the right person for the job of commenting on happiness and joy. After all, I have been quite unimpressed with the fleeting happiness I have managed to corral. Indeed, it is unclear to what extent I am capable of the pursuit of happiness. Going even deeper, into the domain of joy, is generally well beyond my recent experience. As such, my voice on the matter is suspect.

Fortunately, it seems one's lack of expertise on these matters does not preclude their consideration. In fact, it might prove helpful. Consider, for example, Schopenhauer's definition of happiness: "The alleviation of suffering." Adhering to this definition might have one wearing three-sizes-too-small shoes all day for the happiness that results when removing them at day's end. Yet the German philosopher wrote splendidly about the human condition and the pursuit of meaning.

For me -- and admittedly perhaps only for me -- joy is possible even though happiness is elusive. I have experienced deeply meaningful periods of joy while pondering my place in the time-space continuum. Joy comes in the form of relationships, with or without sex, including my relationship to the natural world. Joy comes in the form of nature itself, including the flap of a wing and the song of a bird. I am not particularly happy about my destructive role in this horrifying culture, nor with my current lot in life. Nonetheless, joy has not completely escaped my grasp.

I know that the birds have grown silent in the woods, as pointed out by American poet and professor of poetry Robert Hass in "After Goethe":

*"The birds are silent in the woods.*
*Just wait: soon enough*
*You will be quiet too."*

I know that very soon I will be silent, too. Further, I understand the source of the predicaments driving me over the abyss, and my limited role in their creation. Yet, I am not without joy.

According to numerous media sources, many climate scientists who are paying attention to the predicament in which we are embroiled are depressed. As knowledgeable as most of them, as powerless as each of them, I am still not plagued by depression. Few climate scientists are willing to admit our near-term extinction, doubtless because they lack sufficient background in biology and ecology, and yet they are devastated that the murderous civilization they love is threatened by climate change. My conclusion is far direr, yet my response is muted in comparison.

Perhaps the typical climate scientist finally has realized that we cannot rely upon corporate entities, such as governments, to address climate change. Perhaps this comes as a surprise, hence a source of depression. I am not so naive. A long-time anarchist who gave up on large entities decades ago, I am more amused than depressed at the absence of a serious effort rooted in civilization to deal with a predicament created by civilization. I am fully aware that abrupt climate change is hardly the only route to near-term human extinction, each of which we are rabidly pursuing.

Of course we are going to die. Of course *Homo sapiens* will go extinct. Of course this is happening faster than expected. Of course irrational people will assume otherwise, and promote belief over evidence in resisting reality.

The birds have grown silent in the woods. Soon, as one consequence, we will be silent, too.

## *Our Terminal Diagnosis*

Imagine receiving a terminal diagnosis at a young age. You might be simultaneously liberated and devastated. You are suddenly able to live as you like, freed from the shackles of societal expectations. Yet you have no future. Your dreams are shattered. Why bother pursuing excellence and love if you have only weeks or months to live?

This is the predicament we face. It is particularly poignant for those who have been told, and falsely continue to believe, that their dreams will be fulfilled if they work hard and adhere to societal expectations.

Millennials come immediately to mind: They almost universally know they have been gaslighted at the level of the entire society, yet there is no chance for the payoff they have been promised. "Life sucks and then you die" has never had more meaning than for college students wracked with nightmarish debt and pockets full of dreams.

Finding one's meaning in an ambivalent universe is one thing. After all, one's authentic purpose must come from within and it might take years to discover. Finding one's meaning on an indifferent planet rapidly running out of habitat for humans is the ultimate raw deal. It is as if you have worked tirelessly to become the greatest sound engineer in the world immediately before every sentient organism, including you, loses its hearing.

I interacted with many millennials at my home in Belize, where our mission was to facilitate the personal growth of all who visited or lived here. We shared work and meals. We talked until my early bedtime, shortly after an early supper. They knew, even before meeting me, that my generation had crapped on theirs and then lied about it. They know the lies continue, too. My evidence-based confirmation came as no surprise to these extraordinary people who had already chosen a path well beyond that of their ordinary contemporaries.

The response to new information varied, of course. Most visitors stayed as long as they had originally planned. They left on schedule, informed and appreciative. The occasional guest planned an immediate departure, choosing to spend the short time remaining with ailing family members. A few guests arrived alone and departed with a partner. My messages of love and urgency provided inspiration for the urgent love of these latter young-at-heart individuals.

My advice, not that you asked, is to do what seems right for the particular situation without attachment to the outcome. I recommend forsaking hope and fear and instead pursuing action. I recommend living as if death draws near while still flossing and brushing. I recommend adventurous radicalism without intentional harm to oneself or others.

The short version of my advice is contained within three whispered words: Live here now (with an obvious, heartfelt nod to Ram Dass's great book, *Be Here Now*). I realize the inherent difficulty of living fully in the current moment. I also know none of us were ever promised another day. Here and now are all we have and all we have ever had. Were I inclined to believe in miracles, I would call each of us a miracle, considering the odds against any one of us being here at all.

None of my advice will prove easy to implement. Nor should it. Were it easy, anybody could do it. If you are reading these words, then you are definitely not just anybody. As a result, perhaps my advice is what you have come to expect from me:

I am asked nearly every day for advice about living. I recommend living fully. I recommend living with intention. I recommend living urgently, with death in mind. I recommend the pursuit of excellence. I recommend the pursuit of love. It is small wonder I am often derided, mocked, rejected, and isolated by my contemporaries in the scientific community.

In light of the short time remaining in your life, and my own, I still recommend all of the above, even louder than before. More fully than you can imagine. To the limits of this restrictive culture and beyond.

For you. For me. For us. For now.

Live large. Be you, and bolder than you have ever been. Live as if you are dying. Because you are.

No blame, no shame, no judgment of how others live. At the edge of extinction, only love remains.

I know this is a lot to ask. Expressing the best of humanity is quite a task. At this point, though, what have we got to lose?

In short, I recommend the advice given by German-American poet Charles Bukowski in his poem, "roll the dice": "Go all the way." In my experience, it is worth the extremely high cost to fully live.

I have often been too timid in my life, with my predictions, and in the advice I have offered. I have lived on the edge, relative to my cultural contemporaries. It has not been enough. It is still not enough.

I have not gone three or four days without eating, as Bukowski had. I have not frozen on a park bench, as Bukowski had. I have not been jailed, as Bukowski had (although I have taught poetry in jail).

Actually, I was born into captivity, along with my cultural contemporaries. I gleefully entered the indoctrination facilities of public education, believing they would set me free. As an adult, I used the expectations of others as bars to reinforce my confinement. For too long, I failed to recognize the cage surrounding me. Beyond the bounds of societal and cultural indoctrination, I am mostly free, finally.

I am freer than most people I know. I am free to think. I live at the edge of society, dipping in only as necessary. I peek in primarily as a reminder of the horrors. My lenses are insufficient to allow extended views of the misery of contemporary society, overwhelmingly invisible to an overwhelming majority of my contemporaries.

I have experienced derision, mockery, rejection, and intense isolation, as had Bukowski. Physical isolation is a gift, although it took me a long while in the desert to realize it. Intellectual isolation is a curse. Lacking peers is painful, and I am peerless with respect to my professional calling. Yet I do not suffer.

Pain is requisite for thoughtful individuals. Suffering is optional, as allowed by enlightenment. Distinguishing personality from reality is key, as is separating factual evidence from one's personal, emotional response to the evidence. Both tasks are a few steps beyond the vast majority of individuals in a purposely dumbed-down culture dominated by willful ignorance.

Opinions are not evidence, even when the opinions are provided by celebrities. My own acceptance of evidence has engendered my liberation. I am not alone, judging from the appreciative messages I receive each day.

## Responding to Our Terminal Diagnosis

I am often accused of encouraging people who follow my work to pursue hedonism. Alternately, I am occasionally accused of causing the suicide of somebody who reads my writing or hears me speak. There seems no middle ground.

Gonzo journalist Hunter S. Thompson is renowned for his line, "I hate to advocate drugs, alcohol, violence, or insanity to anyone, but they've always worked for me."

Hedonism, according to the definitions in my dictionary, include (1) the doctrine that pleasure or happiness is the sole or chief good in life, and (2) a way of life based on or suggesting the principles of hedonism.

Please do not misinterpret me. I am hardly a prude. I am a huge fan of pleasure. I have no problem with happiness, as long as it is not confused with joy or acquisition of material possessions. Hedonism seems a few materialistic steps beyond pleasure, perhaps into the realm of ecstasy. I love feeling ecstatic.

The issue is clearly one of degree. I suspect we enter difficult ethical terrain when pleasure becomes *the sole or chief good in life.* Defining moderation, as sought by Socrates, is a worthy pursuit (ditto for the remaining handful of Socrates' pursuits, namely justice, good, virtue, piety, and courage). The ancient expression, "nothing too much" -- unfortunately twisted into the contemporary phrase, "moderation in all things," -- has great merit.

I am often asked if my message will not lead people down the path of hedonism. My standard response is to ask when hedonism has been recently forsaken in the country of my birth. Most members of the privileged audience believe I am joking. A short time later, we turn out the lights and the people in the audience drive home, stopping only for a quick bite to eat in one of the restaurants they pass on the way to their two-car garage in suburbia.

When did irony die? Did I miss the celebration of life, which used to be called a funeral?

Most people claim, contrary to Gonzo's quote, that they detest violence. Yet these same people benefit from, and apparently appreciate, the oppression and early deaths of people who happen to live in the vicinity of fossil fuels requisite to maintenance of American Empire.

The aforementioned line from long-dead American comedian Bill Hicks with respect to caffeine and alcohol is fitting. These are the drugs Thompson claimed he appreciated, in his clever, insightful manner. I suspect he agreed with Hicks, although we will probably never know.

So much for violence and drugs. What about insanity?

What more can I write or say about a culture gone mad? I have written thousands of words in dozens of essays about individual and societal madness. For more than two decades, I have predicted an acceleration of violence as economic contraction proceeds. Yet the mad march on, believing themselves sane because their indoctrination is so stunningly complete.

There is no external escape. There is no place to hide. Only by introspection can one escape the madness of contemporary culture.

No drugs needed. You can skip the violence, too.

# Chapter 7: A Synopsis

*The mystery of human existence lies not in just staying alive, but in finding something to live for*

(Fyodor Dostoevsky)

American evolutionary biologist George C. Williams died in September, 2010 at the age of 83 years. I doubt he knew we were facing our own imminent extinction when he wrote, "Most evolving lineages, human or otherwise, when threatened with extinction, don't do anything special to avoid it."

By the time Williams died, I had been sounding the alarm at guymcpherson.com for three years. I was hardly alone. The warnings I will mention in this short summary were hardly the first ones about climate catastrophe likely to result from burning fossil fuels. A little time with your favorite online search engine will take you to George Perkins Marsh sounding the alarm in 1847, Svente Arrhenius's relevant journal article in 1896, and young versions of Al Gore, Carl Sagan, and James Hansen testifying before the United States Congress in the 1980s. There is more, of course, all ignored for a few dollars in a few pockets.

The projected rate of climate change based on IPCC-style gradualism outstrips the adaptive response of vertebrates by a factor of 10,000 times, as mentioned in an earlier chapter. Even closer to *Homo sapiens*, mammals cannot evolve fast enough to escape the current extinction crisis. Humans are vertebrate mammals. To believe that our species can avoid extinction, even as non-human vertebrates and non-human mammals disappear, is classic human hubris wrapped in a warm blanket of myth-based human supremacy. The evidence indicates humans will join the annihilation of "all life on earth," as reported in the journal *Scientific Reports* on 13 November 2018. After all, humans are alive (some more than others).

The catastrophic, uncontrolled meltdown of the world's nuclear power facilities is sufficient, but not necessary, for the near-term loss of life on Earth. "Only" abrupt climate change is necessary to rid Earth of all life.

The response to these warnings, throughout history? Shift the baseline. Ignore the abundant science. Throw caution to the wind.

The corporate media, governments, and most climate scientists continue to adhere to the 2°C target proposed by economist William Nordhaus in 1977: "If there were global temperatures more than 2°C or 3°C above the current average temperature, this would take the climate outside of the range of observations which have been made over the last several hundred thousand years."

We know quite a bit more about climate science than we did in 1977. Real scientists knew, even way back then, that economists were not to be treated as scientists. It is small wonder Nordhaus shared the politically motivated Nobel Prize in Economics in 2018. I would not have been surprised had he been given the Nobel Peace Prize, thus joining fellow specialists-in-genocide Henry Kissinger and Barack Obama.

Earth is currently at least 1.73°C above the 1750 baseline marking the beginning of the Industrial Revolution. This global-average temperature is the highest ever with *Homo sapiens* present, according to a 2017 paper in *Earth System Dynamics* by James Hansen and colleagues. In other words, our species has never experienced a hotter Earth than the one currently driving the ongoing refugee crisis as habitat for humans disappears. Earth is not quite at the 2°C limit established by Nordhaus.

In response to the ever-accelerating crisis known as abrupt climate change, the conventional approach is to shift the baseline. Instead of admitting the planet is nearly 2°C above the 1750 baseline, governments and many scientists have determined the baseline is actually 1981-2010, or later. Adherence to the Precautionary Principle is clearly unfashionable.

We have known for decades that the 2°C number set in stone by Nordhaus is dangerous. According to a 1965 speech by Frank Ikard, chief of the American Petroleum Institute, "time is running out" to deal with the effects of climate change. In late June, 1989, Noel Brown, the director of the New York office of the United Nations

Environment Program, indicated we had only until 2000 to avoid catastrophic climate change. About 16 months after Brown's warning, the United Nations *Advisory Group on Greenhouse Gases* set 1°C as the absolute upper limit in October, 1990. Climate speaker and writer David Spratt said 0.5°C was the absolute upper limit in October, 2014.

It was almost certainly too late to reverse abrupt, irreversible climate change in 1977 when Nordhaus shared his genocidal opinion. It certainly was too late to change course in 1989. Comforting words and future promises aside, we have not done anything to prevent our own extinction in the wake of warnings distant or near.

In October, 2018, the United Nation's Intergovernmental Panel on Climate Change indicated we have until 2030 to hold global-average temperature at 1.5°C above the ever-shifting baseline. Yes, that is correct: The United Nations is recommending a global-average temperature well below the current temperature as a "target."

It gets worse, of course: In September, 2018, United Nations Secretary-General António Guterres was widely quoted as saying we have until 2020 to turn this ship around. The only known means by which humans can change the global-average temperature in any direction between now and 2020 is the reduction of industrial activity, which will alleviate the aerosol masking effect and therefore drive the global-average much higher very quickly. That definitely is not the direction we want the temperature to change if we are interested in maintaining habitat for vertebrates and mammals on Earth. Loss of the aerosol masking effect means loss of habitat for human animals, with human extinction to follow.

It gets unimaginably worse by the day, of course. The latest information from the peer-reviewed journal *Literature* finally caught up to me in concluding the Sixth Mass Extinction could annihilate all life on Earth. A paper in the 13 November 2018 edition of *Scientific Reports* by Strona and Bradshaw titled, "Co-extinctions annihilate planetary life during extreme environmental change" draws this conclusion based upon the rapid rate of environmental change, consistent with my own conclusions during the last several years. As one who loves life, my gratification regarding my message from this most conservative of sources is overwhelmed by my sadness at the loss.

To put it simply, our fate as a species is sealed. We are headed for extinction in the very near term despite warnings dating back more than 150 years. It is a tragic tale. As foretold by evolutionary biologist George C. Williams, our species hardly made a squeak as the hammer dropped.

Our time on Earth is short. We are nearing the end of our individual lives. We are nearing the end of the American Empire. We are nearing the end of human life on Earth as well. In response to this knowledge, what are you going to do?

Regular followers of my work know my general responses to this question, responses that focus on the pursuit of a life rich in purpose. I encourage the pursuits of love and excellence. I discourage attachment to the outcome of one's actions. I have been promulgating these messages for several years.

I observe plenty of people chasing what I believe are relatively shallow pursuits when they accept the finitude of life. Some of these people exhibit behaviors consistent with "signaling." These behaviors include, for example, tasting a new variety of wine each night, having passports stamped in many countries, having sex with as many different people as possible, and generally adding variety to what bird-watchers would call "life lists."

I am a huge fan of traveling, particularly when it involves new cultural experiences. I encouraged students in my classrooms to seek such experiences via travel. As I pointed out often, one need not travel via airline to another country to witness a different culture from one's own. Only a few miles from the campus in Tucson, Arizona where I spent most of my academic career were a few cultures markedly different from the ones usually experienced by my students. They are found on lands called, "Indian reservations," a two-word phrase with which I take issue with only two of the words: "Indian" and "reservation."

In the 1980s, and likely during other times, "living large" meant hookers and blow. I have tried neither prostitutes nor cocaine, and I am judgmental about neither your sex life nor your choice of drugs (including alcohol). However, I have long wondered if the pursuit of happiness is worthy. Perhaps a deeper satisfaction can be found by pursuing joy instead of happiness, an idea I have pondered often. For example, I suspect -- although I certainly cannot know, not for everyone -- that William Blake's "eternity in an hour" is more likely to be found in intimacy than in sex. Wine is fine, and introspection is often finer (full disclosure: I generally do not like wine). Perhaps there is more lasting meaning in the gratitude of a small, local life than in the hookers-and-blow version of "living large."

I do not know your circumstances. If they resemble mine, they change frequently. I recognize and appreciate the difficulty in seeking meaning, much less joy, when the pursuits of water, food, and shelter are constant preoccupations. Been there, done that, and could not even afford the tee shirt.

I also know that valid insights contributing to meaning can spring from impoverishment. The Buddha and Gandhi come to mind. I would mention contemporary figures were it not for concerns about privacy as well as the judgmental perception of hubris and humility.

Life is short. Life is difficult. We have all witnessed the feebleness described by British philosopher Bertrand Russell.

Courage demands we act in accordance with reality. Although life is short and difficult, it is beautiful and often even worthy as well.

Pleasure is easy to obtain, at least temporarily. Joy is difficult to capture. Perhaps this is why some of us prefer joy.

# Chapter 8: Passionately Pursuing a Life of Excellence

*We are what we repeatedly do. Excellence, then, is not an act, but a habit.*

(Aristotle)

## *Mundane Matters*

I know only one poem written by British poet Frances Darwin Cornford, granddaughter of Charles Darwin. I find this particular poem provocative. It is titled, "Youth," and it describes the difficulty of the daily grind of life:

> *A young Apollo, golden-haired,*
> *Stands dreaming on the verge of strife,*
> *Magnificently unprepared*
> *For the long littleness of life.*

I thought I was going to positively change the world. I suspect most of us once believed we were the golden-haired Apollos exquisitely described by Cornford. I suspect most of us who find ourselves surprisingly well into their second semi-centennial, as I do, identify with Cornford's "long littleness of life."

Living with urgency, as I often recommend, is challenging. It requires focused attention. It is therefore exhausting. Why bother?

Why bother being consumed by Cornford's "long littleness of life," which I interpret as diligently attending to the mundane details of daily living? Why bother living with urgency? Why bother paying attention? Why bother being fully present? Why bother living in the here and now?

These are great questions. As I told my students in classrooms for two decades, when I say, "That's a great question," it means I do not have a definitive answer.

Why bother? So far, at least for me, the alternative to the long littleness of life is not appealing. So far, at least for me, the certainty of my near-term death, coupled with the absurdity of life, encourages me to march onward through the mundane details of everyday life. Better yet, my Camus-inspired perspective regarding absurdity and my Edward Abbey-inspired sense of anarchism allow me to appreciate the mundane details of my daily life. Perhaps an example will help.

I used to rush through the mundane tasks I deemed important only in the sense that they illustrated my desire to take responsibility for myself. I would take out the garbage, wash laundry, and clean the countertop with an uninspired approach: Must Go Faster (MGF). Now, however, I am less hurried and more attentive as I go about these tasks. Just a little while ago,

I gathered the garbage in the apartment I occupy and then I hauled it to the nearby dumpster. It went swimmingly, so I will tell you all about it.

Four baskets were filled with garbage from the three rooms upstairs. How did that happen? Included was the package from the crackers I had two days ago for lunch. The package made me smile, and it took me back to yesterday's light breakfast, no lunch, and then dinner with two beautiful new friends. I look forward to seeing the friends again in the days ahead. Doing so will interfere with my ability to research, synthesize, and promulgate evidence about our imminent demise. This tradeoff is definitely worth it.

Downstairs were three trash containers, including the big one in the kitchen. It reeked of rotten bananas. I love the smell of bananas, even rotten ones. I carefully put all the trash, from upstairs and down, into a total of four bags. I exchanged the slippers on my feet for slip-on shoes and ventured into the freezing outdoors. I know it was freezing because the snow that fell early this morning is still about an inch deep on the sidewalk. My arms full, I stopped to smell the crisp outdoor air before proceeding to the dumpster. Then I leisurely returned to my keyboard. I could go on, as regular readers know, describing the falling of each footstep, the sounds of the village, and my focused attention to each breath. With this mundane task, I was balancing urgency with a profound appreciation for the mundane that I formerly lacked. I am now urgently, diligently paying attention to details that I ignored for more than five decades.

I enjoyed the 10-minute excursion even as my MGF non-consciousness was whispering that I could have accomplished the task in half the time. Yes, I argued with my MGF non-consciousness, but the five minutes saved would not have been worth it. I have traded in the ability to accomplish more work for the appreciation of the here and now.

Even if I exceed my anticipated expiration date by a few years, I have very few remaining trips to the dumpster. I will not get to take out the trash more than a few dozen times. I will revel in every one. I will gladly dismiss thoughts of Must Go Faster for a few more breaths of crisp air.

## Hope is a Mistake and a Lie

The ongoing, seemingly endless cries for hope indicate we have entered desperate times. After all, hope – in the absence of the possibility of success -- is a mistake and a lie. In such circumstances, clinging to hope is a mistake, and promulgating hope is a lie.

I have pointed out repeatedly that wishing for a positive future is a mistake when success is beyond our reach. After all, hope in such circumstances is wishful thinking that assumes a positive future without supporting evidence. Hope and fear are the twin sides of the same coin, and the coin assumes *others* will fix whatever is broken. Sadly, there is no "fix" for the predicament known as abrupt, irreversible climate change.

I prefer action over hope or fear, so, I take action. From my days as a homesteader, a project initiated in 2007, I have taken radical actions that might have mattered with respect to slowing or stopping abrupt climate change and the Sixth Mass Extinction had they been pursued by many people decades before I naively started. I have been routinely disparaged for these actions, and they were followed far too late and by too few people to make a difference. Thus do we find *Homo sapiens* embroiled within the Sixth Mass Extinction triggered by abrupt climate change.

Lacking the possibility of success, hope is not only a mistake, it is also a lie. Consistent with many of the lies we have been told, we have accepted the lie of hope for so long we no longer recognize it as a lie. As victims of industrial civilization, we prefer the comfortable lie to the bitter truth. We love our comforts, and the lie of hope makes us better able to "fit in" with the majority of other members within our diseased society.

Hope, without even the slimmest possibility of success, is to believe in a favorable future without evidence. It is based on faith. Faith requires no evidence. Indeed, evidence generally interferes with faith: witness the spiritually religious among us.

The faith-based junk science known as belief in a favorable future (i.e., hope with no possibility of success) presents significant impediments to a rational approach, as pointed out in a paper by Rogers and colleagues in the 3 August 2017 issue of the peer-reviewed journal, *Psychological Science* ("The Belief in a Positive Future").

For example, according to the senior author of the peer-reviewed paper in an interview coincident with the release of the paper, "Belief in a favorable future may diminish the likelihood that people will take action to ensure that the favorable future becomes reality." In short, the evidence indicates hope, like fear, is a terrible idea.

If you are forced to choose between hope and fear, I suspect you know which of the two is more likely to inspire rapid, radical action. The Manhattan Project during World War II serves as an example.

When the infamous 300 of Sparta faced off against the thousands of Persians at the Hotgates/Thermopylae, they knew there was no hope. The Spartans said their goodbyes to their comrades, families, and lovers and took action. They were not going down without a fight, without hurting the invaders before their ill-gotten victory. These 300 Spartans knew there was no escape for them. They knew it was very unlikely the Athenians would show up to support them. They knew their number was up, that their wives, children, and lands would be pillaged and raped. And yet, despite what we hear in current mainstream media about hope being the ideal approach, versus accepting the inevitable outcome of being doomed, or the tripe that denying people hope kills one's sense of urgency, which is not only a bald-faced lie, but has been proven wrong in scientific research, these 300 Spartans fought to the very last and gave the Persians a day to remember. They gave us all a day to remember, along with the deepest understanding that hope is not necessary to fight tooth and nail to one's last breath, to the last standing man or woman. Hope is a waste of time at the edge of extinction.

The Israelite residents of Masada also knew hope was a lie. They had no doubt that their lifestyle, customs, and lives would be destroyed when the Romans arrived. The Romans were good at creating slave labor and reducing entire, proud nations down to scullery levels. The Roman reputation of subsuming entire cultures into the murderous, Roman civilization preceded it. The Israelites were not going down without a fight, albeit a different kind of fight. They removed themselves from their inevitable destiny of being reduced to mere human resources for the Romans. They committed mass suicide, an act of pure heroism and courage and of spitting in the face of unimpeachable odds. They rejected hope as a fool's option and seized action as their antidote to despair.

Moving ahead a few centuries, most of us know how positivity worked for the French Revolutionaries. They did not have a festival to celebrate how cool it would be for the rich aristocrats to share their wealth, and they did not perform street theater about their wishes. They did not write funny songs to bring smiles to people's faces. They recognized they were screwed if they did nothing and that they, therefore, had nothing to lose. They took what they needed by force, not with pretty speeches or petitions. Not with begging each other to be peaceful or hopeful, but demanding everyone fight for what was decent and necessary. There was blood and no hope, and they won.

For the most part, hope is a lie, a mistaken dream, or a wish for a different outcome. Hope betrays the warrior within us and embraces the complacency that A *Deus Ex Machina* will arrive to rescue us. Hope sees us waiting, lost in a dream of our own invention, hands clasped in prayer and longing, immobilized and impotent, incapable of true action or genuine thought.

News flash! There is no Superman coming. There is no god coming. There are no aliens coming. There is no planet X coming back around to set things straight. This is it. We are it. We are our own heroes and our own mass murderers. We can accept the cold, hard truth like the Spartans did and stand fiercely against what comes, or we can daydream away our last days with hope in the form of "fix-it" rubbish such as Transition Towns, permaculture, veganism, praying, being positive, or blaming politicians. Abrupt climate change is here, the aerosol masking effect is here, the methane bomb has gone off, there is no way to escape this jewel of a planet that we turned into a prison and a death trap for all our non-human relatives.

Put your misplaced hope where it belongs, in the dustbin of terrible ideas, and face the future with courage, love, and a sense of being present. We can act as those 300 Spartans did, digging their sun-kissed heels hard into the Earth that bore them and that would presently take their lifeblood back. Every breeze that touched their burning flesh was a kiss, the sun upon their helmets was a warm caress, the weight of their steel in their hands a comforting and familiar heft, the sound of their brother's breathing at their sides and their deep voices a balm upon their ears. Every last breath and sight and sound was a treasure to remember as long as there was life in their bones. They could live fully, honestly, with good character even as life was taken from them. They had no hope and they were the best humans they had ever been.

Sadly, the idea of hope has been imposed upon this culture as a necessity for our wellbeing. Hope has been deemed unimpeachably good. Perhaps this is because hope is imperative if the masses are to be kept in their corral. Even exploiting hope-filled youngsters such as Greta Thunberg in December, 2018 to keep the house of cards intact via heartfelt video, more or less, is nothing new (the same trick was played on us using Severn Cullis-Suzuki in December, 1992).

It ought to come as no surprise that hope has become a religion as powerful as Catholicism during The Crusades. After all, there is nothing to be done about abrupt, irreversible climate change except keeping the show going for as long as money can buy pleasure. Promulgating hope is part of the show for which we inherited front-row seats.

I am not suggesting you give up on hope if there is any possibility of success, however slim. Hope is often presented as a positive emotion even when there is no possibility of success, and it is in these cases that hope is a mistake. After all, we learn from our mistakes. As a teacher, I would hate to interfere with your educational process.

The living planet is in the fourth and final stage of a terminal disease. Hope will not stave off the Sixth Mass Extinction. Hope will neither slow nor stop human extinction. It is long past time we admitted hospice is the appropriate way forward.

Regular readers of my work might recall a time I was routinely assailed for not "joining forces" with the likes of Bill McKibben and his ilk. I pointed out McKibben was lying about climate change long before it was fashionable to do so. He became a well-known entity in a short period of time. He and his organization were funded by the Rockefeller Foundation (aka Big Oil). McKibben made a name for himself, and apparently a lot of money, by taking the customary, halfway approach with the evidence. His fans and many other people accused me of "stealing hope" and "giving up." I was not, and am not, interested in capitulating to irrational thinking. I prefer adherence to principle over being paid to generate confusion.

Now I am often told I need to support the Extinction Rebellion (XR). I am told XR is transmitting the same message I have been promulgating (they are not). I am further informed they are promoting my work (in a culture of profound ignorance and rampant dumbassery, *denying* my work is perceived as *promoting* my work. XR is making a name for itself and has become a well-known entity in a short period of time. They take the customary, halfway approach with the evidence (evidence that I have provided for them and that they give me no credit for. In fact, many members do not even know who I am). I keep pointing out that XR is ignoring the aerosol masking effect, and that rebelling against extinction is analogous to rebelling against the sunrise. In return, members of the group routinely trash me for "stealing hope" and "giving up." I would add only that, with respect to human extinction, the rebellion against sunrise is beginning at high noon.

You might see similarities in these two cases claiming that I must get on board with the likes of McKibben and also XR. I see them.

I suspect I have sacrificed more than McKibben and the entire, combined passel of folks involved in the XR movement. Yet I am painted as the criminal for "stealing hope" (whatever that means) and "giving up" (whatever that means). Apparently presenting the full evidence about abrupt climate change makes me the bad person in a culture infatuated with magical thinking. Apparently, the customary, halfway approach is preferred because it allows the retention of hope and the perception that something is being done (by somebody else).

In a ploy that dates to biblical times, those working on behalf of the dominant paradigm continue to kill evidentiary messengers while co-opting their message. My own ability to transmit my message has been destroyed by both the assassins and their propaganda. My teachings are now being cunningly marketed by the same group of people I spoke against, this time to reinforce the status quo.

Notwithstanding the ongoing attempt to assassinate my character, hope is still a mistake, as I have pointed out repeatedly in my essays and presentations. Hope is not only a mistake: Hope is a lie. Of course, most of us refuse to believe hope is a lie because that would require us to admit we lie to ourselves. As Mark Twain indicated, "It's easier to fool people than to convince them that they have been fooled." Few want to admit they have been fooled, so they continue to lie about their foolishness. There is no finer set of fools than those who believe in a favorable future in the midst of abrupt, irreversible climate change.

Contrary to hope, love requires honesty. Love means telling the full truth and acting on that truth, not the customary, halfway version. A loving relationship requires honesty and honest action, not hope.

Perhaps hope is a disease. Perhaps Willard and Marguerite Beecher were correct in their 1965 book, *Beyond Success and Failure:*

> *Hope is a whore, a cheat, a deceiver. She seduces victims and makes unwarranted, ungrounded promises so that they lean on her-not on themselves. Hope is merely wishful thinking, or longing, for Santa Claus to bail us out. Hope entices us to postpone living in the present as if there were a future on which we could depend. The more one depends on hope, the more one fears for his situation. Hope deferred dries up like a raisin in the sun. When Pandora opened the box of evils-war, pestilence, disease, famine and all their kin emerged to flood*

*the world. The greatest evil came out last.
It was hope-the great postponer, the
tempter to abdication, the deathblow to
initiative. Hope is a fear of the present.*

Perhaps love is the cure. I doubt we persist long
enough to perform the relevant research to find out.

The living planet is in the fourth and final stage of
a terminal disease. As I have pointed out for several years,
it is long past time we admitted hospice is the only
reasonable way forward.

# Chapter 9: Between Two Dreams

*Any good poet, in our age at least, must begin with the scientific view of the world; and any scientist worth listening to must be something of a poet, must possess the ability to communicate to the rest of us their sense of love and wonder at what their work discovers.*

(Edward Abbey)

True to the idea of living my message, I conclude this short text with lyrics I've written. I would love to have a musician write music to accompany my lyrics and make them into a real song. I offer it in the spirit of Edward Abbey, the long-time, Tucson-based writer who so influenced me.

My simple writing is hardly great art. That is not the point, as you have likely gathered by now.

# Wilderness of Love

By Guy McPherson and Kelly Goodlad

Everybody knows that
We can't live forever
But few can comprehend
Humanity's end

We fight to make a living
So busy we don't see the dying
Of the trees and birds and oceans
And every living thing

Chorus:

I've found my own way
It's not along some highway
Beyond all the byways
Sometimes a lonely road

In the wilderness of my dreams
In the wilderness of your dreams
In the wilderness of our dreams
The wilderness of love

*Born into captivity*
*Believing that you're free*
*In this "civilized society"*
*Behind bars you can't see*

*With urgency I'm living*
*I've got a sense that we're dying*
*So I throw off these shackles*
*And grasp at my dreams*

*Chorus*

*Nothing left to lose*
*Means everything to gain now*
*Living on the edge*
*Means going all the way*

*There's no more to fear*
*We're in the final lap now*
*The Sixth Mass Extinction*
*Means we're going away*

*Chorus*

# About the Author

Guy R. McPherson is an internationally recognized speaker, award-winning scientist, and the world's foremost authority on abrupt climate change leading to near-term human extinction. He is Professor Emeritus at the University of Arizona, where he taught and conducted research for twenty years. His published works include more than a dozen books and hundreds of scholarly articles.

Dr. McPherson has been featured on television and radio and in several documentary films. He is a public speaker, blogger, cultural critic, and the long-time co-host of his own radio show *Nature Bats Last* on the Progressive Radio Network. He was certified by the Grief Recovery Institute as a grief-recovery specialist (not a counselor) in January, 2014.

He currently lives in New York state.